The Reform of
Social Security

The Reform of Social Security

A. W. Dilnot, J. A. Kay, and C. N. Morris

The Institute for Fiscal Studies
London

CLARENDON PRESS · OXFORD
1984

Oxford University Press, Walton Street, Oxford OX2 6DP

London New York Toronto
Delhi Bombay Calcutta Madras Karachi
Kuala Lumpur Singapore Hong Kong Tokyo
Nairobi Dar es Salaam Cape Town
Melbourne Auckland

and associated companies in
Beirut Berlin Ibadan Mexico City Nicosia

Oxford is a trade mark of Oxford University Press

Published in the United States
by Oxford University Press, New York

British Library Cataloguing in Publication Data
Dilnot, A.W.
The reform of social security.
1. Social security – Great Britain
I. Title   II. Kay, J.A.   III. Morris, C.N.
368.4'00941   HD7165
ISBN 0-19-877226-2
ISBN 0-19-877225-4 Pbk

Set by Hope Services, Abingdon
Printed in Great Britain by
Biddles Ltd, Guildford.

Preface

The work carried out for this book forms part of the Institute for Fiscal Studies (IFS) project on the Distributional Effects of Fiscal Policy, which is financed by the Gatsby Foundation. Later stages of the research were supported by the Economic and Social Research Council. The Family Expenditure Survey data on which much of the analysis is based were provided by the Department of Employment. We are very grateful to these organisations.

We are also very grateful to members of the IFS staff and to other individuals who have provided helpful comments and advice, and in particular to Les Hannah, James Meade, Marion Morris, Barbara Rodgers and Clive Smee for detailed comments on previous drafts; to Martha Holmes, Barbara Lee, Cathy Pearcey, and Siân Turner for the preparation of successive drafts of the typescript; to Graham Richardson and Nicola Spencer for preparing the index, and to Janet Moore for research assistance on the historical section. Any errors remain our own.

Thou source of all my bliss, and all my woe,
That foundst me poor at first, and keepst me so.

Oliver Goldsmith, 'The Deserted Village'.

Contents

List of Figures

List of Tables

Introduction

Social security is 'another British failure'. The home of the welfare state has one of the lowest levels of social benefits and one of the least dynamic economies in the Western world. The British still take some pride in their social institutions. Although our health service and our education system are often criticised, there is widespread support for the basic structure of their organisation and most people in Britain would feel that other countries could learn at least as much from us as we could from them. There is no similar affection for our social security system. If we are reluctant to change, it is not because we are happy with the status quo, but because we lack a convincing critique and a persuasive agenda for reform. It is these that this book sets out to provide.

We begin in Chapter 1 with an account of the evolution of the British social security system, with particular emphasis on the Beveridge Report. The report is a document of remarkable distinction and it continues to exercise a hold on the popular imagination. The purpose of this historical account is not to provide either a comprehensive assessment of the Beveridge Report, or a definitive treatment of the development of British social security policy. To do either of these jobs would fill this volume. Instead, we use it to present the argument that the Beveridge concept of social insurance has proved inadequate as a basis for the British social security system and that it has in fact been substantially abandoned, partly by modifications within the structure of the national insurance scheme itself and partly by the development of an increasingly extensive network of benefits outside it.

Moreover, the concept of social insurance has proved inadequate for reasons which were widely canvassed at the time of the Beveridge Report, and which would emerge again if any serious attempt were made to implement Beveridge principles. One reason is that a comprehensive network of social insurance benefits is simply too expensive. The second is that the principle is insufficiently flexible to meet the variety of individual needs and changing economic circumstances.

The most common response of critics of our social security system is to observe that these difficulties could be overcome if only we were

1

willing to spend more money. This is, in a sense, a correct response. The Beveridge design would work, or work better, if we were willing to fund a wider range of benefits at a higher level. But it is a fact that the will to achieve this has not existed at any time in the last forty years. Nor is this likely to change: the political climate in Britain, and in the Western world generally, is now increasingly hostile to additional social security expenditure. The pressure now is not to spend more on social security but to spend less. It is therefore time to ask how we can more effectively use the resources currently devoted to social security.

If Chapter 1 is a critique of the Beveridge Report, Chapter 2 is a critique of the tax and social security systems as they stand today. The issues involved are by no means the same. The Beveridge Report may provide the intellectual basis of British social security policy but, as in many other areas, the problem is not that policy lacks an intellectual basis but that it has one which is both out of date and substantially unrelated to what we actually do. It is a good deal easier for most people to change what they do than to change what they think, and this is well illustrated by the Department of Health and Social Security (DHSS) official who could still proclaim himself a 'National Insurance man' in spite of the comprehensive retreat from the principles of national insurance which he was ready to describe (Chapter 1, Appendix B).

The criticisms presented in Chapter 2 concern two main groups of issues. One is the inefficiency evident in many parts of the system. This is true in many senses of the word efficiency. Administrative costs are too high, and there is a good deal of unnecessary duplication of activity and effort. Benefits do not go to those who are entitled to them, and do go to those who are not entitled to them, or who should not be entitled to them. Much social security expenditure goes to families and individuals who would not be poor even if they did not receive it. The second set of problems arises from the unplanned interactions of the tax and benefit systems caused by their piecemeal development. The best known of these are the poverty and unemployment traps which affect low-income households.

We go on to argue that an explicit abandonment of the national insurance concept and the pursuit of a single, properly integrated tax and benefit system provide the only promising direction of reform. The tax and benefit systems grew up separately for different groups of people, and under the aegis of different Departments of State. Before the Second World War, those who received benefits and those who paid tax were two distinct groups. The Beveridge Report extended benefits to taxpayers, and rising real incomes brought most benefit recipients into tax. Most households now both receive benefits and pay tax.

In Chapters 3 and 4 we consider how the tax and social security systems might be brought more closely together. The first tentative but practicable scheme of this kind was the tax credit scheme proposed by the Conservative Government in the early 1970s. Our proposals extend this 'tax credit' concept by introducing a number of 'benefit credits' which are withdrawn, through the tax system, from higher-income households. By this means, we bring state support for the children and housing costs of working families into a single framework for assessment and payment which is part of the income tax system. This framework can then be extended to cover the old and the unemployed. We have spelt out the administrative implications of these proposals at some length, although we have not gone so far as to provide a detailed blueprint which could form the basis of immediate implementation. There is no point in doing so until the political will to move in the direction of our reforms is there; but equally, no one can reasonably be expected to summon up that political will unless they are satisfied that the central elements of a set of realisable administrative changes are there. That is the level of analysis which we have sought to provide.

Do our proposals require computerisation? Certainly we assume that both the Revenue and Social Security Departments would wish to make full use of modern technology. Moreover, we take very explicit account of the way in which this technology is changing the nature of the options available to us. Tasks of data handling, information storage and calculation become easier and cheaper year by year, while judgement and discretion become more difficult and more expensive. We think this ought to influence the kind of tax and benefit system which we would want to implement, as well as how we would want to operate the one we have, and we find it extraordinary that this does not seem to have been recognised so far. But while we have tried to be imaginative in finding technical solutions to problems, our proposals do not depend on any great technological leaps forward of the kind which history should make us hesitant to recommend again to the British Government or its agencies. In fact we think that the current computerisation plans of both the Inland Revenue and the DHSS are too elaborate, too ambitious, and too expensive, and are extremely concerned by the fact that they are formulated independently of each other.

In Chapter 4, we use the benefit credit approach to mimic the existing system of direct tax and benefits. This will seem to many a rather pointless exercise. It is unlikely that anyone viewing the British structure of tax and social security from a detached standpoint would wish to implement the existing system of tax and benefits, and we have described in Chapter 2 a number of very persuasive arguments why he should not. There are several reasons for adopting this initial procedure. One is that it demonstrates the flexibility of our design — if it can reproduce more or less exactly the extraordinary pattern of income distribution achieved by our current arrangements, it can do anything. Another more important reason is that we are anxious to separate the issues of administrative and substantive reform. There are too many historical instances, especially in the field of social security, of desirable administrative changes being successfully blocked by those who opposed the associated distributional consequences or distrusted the political motives of those who put them forward. This is exactly what happened to the 1972 tax credit scheme.

A subsidiary purpose of this analysis is to introduce the reader to the IFS tax and benefit models which lie behind our work. These replicate the effects of tax and benefit changes on a case-by-case basis for a sample of 7,525 households, based on profiles derived from the 1981 Family Expenditure Survey. They therefore enable us to identify and describe in detail the gains and losses to individual families from policy reforms. We can show, for example,that under the pattern of benefit credit put forward in Chapter 4 some 88 per cent of working households would obtain net incomes which are between 99 per cent and 101 per cent of their entitlement under present rules and legislation. This capability also enables us to provide accurate costings of our proposals. In addition, we can assess the effect on other factors, such as the incentive to obtain additional earnings or to seek work. As far as we know, no set of tax or benefit proposals put forward in the UK has ever before been analysed in this detailed and comprehensive way, either within government or outside it. This is a necessary background to Chapter 5, where we consider modifications to the system that would affect income distribution, often in radical ways.

In considering changes to the structure of the tax and benefit systems, we have had in mind a number of different objectives. We have sought to reduce expenditure so as to allow substantial tax reductions. We have sought to protect and in general improve the position of poor individuals and households. We have sought to simplify the system. We have tried to rationalise and in general to improve the relationship between incomes in work and those obtained out of work. We are anxious to remove the worst excesses of the poverty trap.

In Chapter 5, we put forward detailed, specific, and costed proposals which meet these objectives within the existing social security budget. The proposals allow for a reduction of five points in the basic rate of income tax — from 30 per cent to 25 per cent — over a band of income somewhat wider than that which applies at present. At the same time, they allocate about £5 billion to improving the position of the worst off — particularly pensioners with no other source of income, and low-income families where the head of the household is in work. The combined effect of these changes and the improvement of take-up by greater automaticity is to reduce by almost half the number of people with incomes below 120 per cent of the present supplementary benefit level.

To achieve all this must sound like magic to those familiar with British social security problems. There is, in fact, no magic. The savings we have effected are achieved by a savage, but selective, retrenchment of the benefit system. It rests on the principle that, as far as better-off households are concerned, provision for children, old age, dependent spouses, and other contingencies is a matter for these households rather than for the state. It therefore abandons the last vestige of the Beveridge plan — the payment of benefit based on potential, rather than actual, need — on the simple, but persuasive, argument that it is very much more cost-effective to tackle actual need. It involves an extension of means testing, in the sense that several benefits which are now paid regardless of income would become related to income. But these additional 'means tests', and some current ones, would be administered through the tax system, and so poor families would in fact be subject to less, and less demeaning, enquiry into their household circumstances than is now the case.

1
History

Beginnings

It is well known that the Beveridge Report proposed, and the post-war Labour Government implemented, the extensive rationalisation of the principle of social insurance which is the cornerstone of the modern social security system. But this report did not occur in a vacuum. It represented the culmination of a process which had been underway for the previous 100 years; the Beveridge Report contained few ideas that were really new. So, to understand its essential characteristics and limitations, we need to look much further back.

The beginning of centralised provision of social security in the UK dates back to the Poor Law Commission of 1834.[1] This, and the subsequent legislation,[2] brought together the administration of a large number of local schemes for provision for the destitute. Yet the Poor Law was a long way from what we mean today by social security. The members of the Commission were less concerned with the alleviation of poverty[3] than with preventing public subsidy of the idle. Able-bodied people were only to be given assistance if they would submit to the rigours of the workhouse, where conditions were set so as to be worse than those faced by the lowest-paid employee.[4] The Poor Law also administered 'outdoor relief' for the sick, disabled and elderly. The principles of the Poor Law remained on the statute book until it was repealed by the Labour Government in 1948.[5]

The late nineteenth century saw a change in attitudes to poverty, and a more contemporary view of the functions of social security began to emerge. The pioneering studies of Charles Booth[6] in London and of Rowntree[7] in York estimated that around 30 per cent of all families were 'without adequate support'. At the same time, it was argued that the major causes of inadequate resources lay not in idleness but in circumstances beyond the control of the individual. Old age, injury at work, sickness, low wages and, towards the end of the century, unemployment accounted for a very high proportion of those in need.[8]

Poverty among those at work was consistently identified as a major cause of poverty from the 1840s onwards. Yet it is only occasionally, and in the main recently, that it has been seen as a policy problem. Aside from its intrinsic significance, it is central to whatever measures are taken to deal with the poverty of the unemployed: only if the net incomes of families with a working head can be kept above a certain level can reasonable benefits be paid to the unemployed without the need to resort to such mechanisms as 'less eligibility' or the 'wage-stop' which attempt to influence directly the relationship between incomes in and out of work.

In the late nineteenth century, there was considerable opposition to the idea of centralised provision of social security. For a very long time, provision for old age had been organised[9] – mainly for richer pensioners – by Friendly Societies, and these saw their position threatened by any state provision. The emerging trade unions were also antagonistic: rudimentary insurance schemes administered by them enhanced their status and power.[10] The charitable organisations, consisting largely of competing churches and temperance societies, also saw their major role threatened by moves towards greater state support.[11] In 1861 the income of charities in London – some £2.5 million – exceeded expenditure under the Poor Law there.[12]

Most Victorian discussion of poverty concerned the position of those of working age. It was assumed that support of the elderly would continue to fall on their families, or on charities. But some critics were specifically concerned with the position of the elderly, and proposals[13] for a fully funded state pension scheme were examined by a Government committee from 1885 to 1887.[14] The fact that Bismarck's Germany had five years previously introduced[15] a system of social insurance for old age enhanced interest. But the power of interested pressure groups[16] was sufficient to prevent any progress. The fundamental political problem, which was to recur again and again over the next century, was that the sacrifices demanded in the present for gains in the future were too great. Not only did a funded scheme which would take at least twenty years to develop require significant current contributions, it also did nothing for those who were already old.

The alternative to a funded insurance basis for pension provision was a non-contributory pension financed from general taxation. When the Royal Commission on the Aged Poor[17] sat in 1895, Denmark already had such a system[18] (since 1891) and New Zealand[19] was soon to follow (1898). In line with the views of the major interested parties, the commission was vigorously opposed to state provision. Another committee sat in 1896,[20] but its terms of reference were carefully drawn up to exclude consideration of non-contributory schemes, and, predictably, it found the political arguments against contributory schemes over-whelming. It was not until 1899, following a strong call from the National Committee of Organised Labour,[21] that a sympathetic com-mittee,[22] under the chairmanship of Henry Chaplin, considered the possibility at all favourably. The recommendations of this committee were for a pension of 5s. a week to be paid to those over 65 with incomes under 10s. and of 'good character' – defined as absence from prison or the workhouse over the preceding twenty years. Although the Boer War and Treasury opposition delayed legislation,[23] the national scheme was implemented from 1910.

The new scheme was based closely on the Chaplin proposals, and has been described by one commentator as 'a scheme for the very old, the very poor and the very respectable'.[24] The pension was to be paid from general taxation and the scheme contained some means-tested elements. The means test was applied to husband and wife and had no regard to the income of the extended family. There were generous income dis-regards, and the fact that the scheme was no longer administered 'by way of the Poor Law' ensured its popularity.

The nineteenth-century approach to social security was dominated by ideas of self-help, but the recognition that the state had a role to play in assisting the unfortunate gradually came to dominate. Some elements in the 1906 Liberal Government wished the state to be much more active in the pursuit of social welfare.[25] Social insurance was a means of reconciling this with a century of *laissez-faire*. The state would provide, but only as a result of the contributions of the individual. The distinction between 'deserving' and 'undeserving' acquired a different basis. So, in 1911, the National Insurance Act[26] introduced compulsory insurance against sickness and unemployment (despite vigorous opposition from the insurance industry, now joined by the medical profession).[27] Coverage for unemployment was limited to only seven industries (carefully selected to minimise the state's risk[28]) and payment was heavily restricted – to fifteen weeks in any year, with the level sufficiently low to discourage malingerers.[29] Despite the limited nature of the provision, the principle of social insurance, which was to become the central theme of the Beveridge Report, was born.

Provision for unemployment appeared of secondary importance at this time. Yet it was the unemployment of the post-war period which nearly destroyed the new system. Unemployment insurance was ex-tended to nearly all the working population in 1920.[30] Following the abolition of wartime controls during 1919-21 and heavy inflation in 1920, unemployment rose steadily to 22 per cent of the insured popu-lation in 1922.

Demands on the system far exceeded its resources, while those whose eligibility had expired because of long periods out of work faced severe hardship. The response was the introduction of a supplementary income-related benefit; by 1933 those on income-related benefits exceeded those covered by insurance.[31] The basic structure of social insurance in practice had emerged. An expensive, but inadequate, scheme of contributory benefits operated in tandem with an extensive non-contributory means-tested system. This was to remain true throughout the next fifty years.

The Beveridge Report was the product of dissatisfaction with the results of these arrangements. The hope was that a post-war world would not face the problems of the 1920s and 1930s and that social insurance could provide adequate provision without the need to resort to means-tested benefits. Beveridge offered a rationalisation of the principle of social insurance, the hope of a comprehensive removal of poverty, and a reaffirmation of the principle of thrift. He added, following a growing awareness of the extent to which large families were at risk from poverty, a commitment to greater support for families with children. Yet history should have led him, and us, to hesitate. The need for the Beveridge Report resulted from the failure of the social insurance principle to meet inter-war economic difficulties. Could it really be the case that the solution lay in a more wholehearted commitment to social insurance? The next forty years were to show that the answer was no.

The Beveridge Report

The Beveridge Report[32] was published in December 1942. The reception it received was, for the most part, an enthusiastic one. The Minister responsible for commissioning it commented that 'no document within living memory has made such a powerful impression, or stirred such hopes, as the Beveridge Report'.[33] In 1944, White Papers[34] accepted its main principles and it formed the basis of post-war legislation on social security. The scheme was firmly based on the concept of social insurance. Beveridge, once an official at the Board of Trade, had been closely involved in the design of the first national insurance scheme and had been an enthusiastic advocate of social insurance ever since.

By social insurance Beveridge meant a system in which all individuals would be liable to make actuarially calculated contributions to a national insurance scheme which would provide cash benefits. These benefits would be sufficient to protect against want in the event of any of the contingencies most likely to lead to poverty – sickness, unemployment, old age, disability, maternity, etc. These arrangements were consciously modelled on private insurance schemes, and indeed Beveridge anticipated that Friendly Societies and trade unions would play a major part in their administration.[35] A safety net of means-tested national assistance would provide for those few whose needs were not met, or not sufficiently met, by insurance benefits.

There were two principal problems. The first was that the scheme was far too expensive. Its immediate costs were formidable; the long-term implications, when rights to benefit had been fully established, were still more serious. The second difficulty was that the principle of social insurance, with benefits related to past contributions rather than current needs, was too rigid to cope with the wide, and changing, range of circumstances which might lead to hardship for individuals and households. Both of these problems were widely recognised at the time of the Beveridge Report itself, by its author and in the extensive debate on the report.[36] Neither was solved. Together, as we show in this chapter, they led to the failure of the Beveridge design.

For Beveridge, the important thing was to establish the principle of social insurance. Financial aspects were essentially secondary, even though daunting. His biographer has written:

Beveridge as a social scientist laid great stress on the need for observation rather than deduction; but this principle had surprisingly little influence on his work as a social reformer. . . For his Social Insurance report Beveridge gathered together a great deal of empirical data; but he used it in exactly the same way as Edwin Chadwick had used empirical data in the famous Poor Law enquiry of 1834 – that is to say, he used it to strengthen the case for policies that he had already chosen on other non-empirical grounds.[37]

The Government Actuary[38] estimated that Beveridge's initial proposals would immediately treble Exchequer expenditure on social security, with very rapid further increases thereafter. He joined with Beveridge, Keynes, and Robbins in a small working group to try to find ways to bring these costs under control. The solution arrived at was a twenty-year transitional period before the planned level of pensions – the most expensive of the proposed benefits – was to be achieved.[39] Over this period, it was assumed, economic growth and contributions paid into the fund would provide resources sufficient to enable the plan to be financed.

The Budget imposes a much increased burden on the Exchequer in later years to provide retirement pensions; this is an act of reasonable faith in the future of the British economic system and the proved efficiency of the British people. That, given reasonable time, this burden can be borne is hardly open to question. The exact rate at which the burden will rise is not settled finally in accepting the plan, since the length of the transition period for pensions is capable of adjustment and, if necessary, can be prolonged without serious hardship.[40]

But economic growth could only ease the burden of providing a given level of benefits if these benefits were not increased in line with increasing incomes — in short, if poverty is defined in absolute terms rather than by reference to the standards of the day. There can be no doubt that this is what Beveridge intended. In the Beveridge Report, poverty is related to physical needs and benefits are to be based on a concept of subsistence income.[41] Although the report acknowledges that standards of subsistence might change over time, the idea of 'relative poverty' — a poverty line which bears some fixed relation to average earnings — was quite alien to Beveridge's conception.

During Beveridge's transitional twenty years — from 1945 to 1965 — prosperity increased at least as rapidly as anyone had anticipated during the war. The absolute standard specified by Beveridge was easily achieved; but expectations and popular conceptions of the poverty line rose as earnings did. To achieve Beveridge's standard of 1942 in 1965 was possible provided there was some growth in the economy. But to achieve that same relative level in 1965 was as difficult as it would have been to achieve his 1942 standard in 1942 — a task which everyone at the time recognised as impossible. In addition, the cost of achieving that relative standard had actually risen considerably

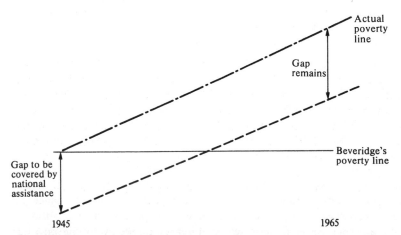

Fig. 1.1. A schematic representation of the transitional period

since Beveridge reported, because the rise in the proportion of pensioners in the population had greatly increased the numbers entitled to benefit. The problem can be seen clearly in Figure 1.1. Beveridge's transitional scheme would, in time, have raised flat-rate benefits to sufficient levels to ensure that all except a small residual category (with abnormal rents, etc.) had incomes above his 'absolute' poverty line. But, during the 1950s and 1960s, demands for a 'relative' poverty line raised the minimum that the state was trying to achieve. National insurance benefits never caught up.

The rising cost of social insurance

The magnitude of potential increases in the cost of social insurance was a major worry from the very beginning. Critical comment[42] on the Beveridge Report was mainly related to the burden which it threatened to impose on future generations. When implemented, benefits were set at a higher initial level than Beveridge proposed, but without his commitment to a gradually increasing benefit level, and the Government made specific provisions[43] for future increases in contributions which would not be related to any increase in benefit.

Table 1.1 shows how costs were expected to develop. The first part is drawn from the Beveridge Report. Over the twenty-year transitional period, they would rise by around 25 per cent. This increase was wholly attributable to the rising burden of retirement pensions. The number of people of pensionable age was expected to increase from 5.6 million (12 per cent of the population) in 1941 to 9.6 million (21 per cent of the population) in 1971. In the event, there were 10.1 million people in this age group in 1971.

An important feature of the Beveridge scheme is that it was intended to cover the whole population, whereas earlier national insurance benefits had been restricted to certain categories of worker.[44] This meant that at the inception of the Beveridge plan there was a substantial group of old people who had little or no existing entitlement to a state pension; but over time virtually everyone of retirement age would acquire such rights.[45] (In 1971 a special non-contributory pension was introduced[46] for the small number who did not.)

Contributions in the Beveridge plan were to be determined actuarially. The weekly amount to be paid was that which would, over a working lifetime, fund the proposed retirement pension and finance the average expected incidence of sickness and unemployment. Although the number of pensioners was to increase markedly in the post-war period, the number of people of working age was actually expected to fall slightly as a result of the low birth rate between the two world wars. The consequence was that a fixed contribution was to be paid by a declining number of people while demands on the fund were rising, and so, as Table 1.2 shows, the Exchequer contribution to the scheme would have to increase substantially.

With contributions actuarially determined, it is at first sight puzzling that the gap between expected inflow and outflow from the scheme is so large. An individual who had contributed to the scheme from the age of 16 would indeed have paid for his pension. But it was to be 1997 before any man would retire who had actually so contributed. Even in maturity, the inflow and outflow from a funded scheme will balance only if the population is in a demographically steady state and the real rate of interest assumed in calculating contributions is zero. But demography was unfavourable,[47] and the Government Actuary was expecting a 2.5 per cent real return[48] on the assets of the National Insurance Fund. In a genuinely funded scheme, this gap would be met by the investment proceeds of the surpluses built up in its early years, when contributions are being paid but accrued rights to pension are very limited. But under the Beveridge proposals, there was to be no cash generated by these means. Instead, there were to be large and growing deficits resulting from the increasing burden of pensions which had, in reality, not been paid for by contributions at any time. There was, therefore, no possibility that contribution income based on the principle of payment for prospective benefits would ever meet any substantial proportion of current benefit expenditure.

The problem is fundamental and recurrent. The provision of pensions through social insurance requires either a very protracted period — fifty years and more — before the scheme reaches maturity; or a rate of contribution which is much in excess of the actual cost of promised benefits; or a large initial subsidy from general taxation. None of these possibilities is ever politically acceptable, and that is why the system is constantly under acute financial pressure. There is an apparent solution to the dilemma. It is to offer ever-increasing benefit levels. The advantage is that you can finance current deficits by current contributions which can be justified by reference to benefits which are not now being paid but will be received in future. The device of meeting yesterday's claims from today's premiums has been familiar to fraudulent and foolish financiers for millenia, and the gaols and workhouses of the world are filled with those private individuals who did not realise that reality breaks through eventually. As we show in the following pages, this is how the Beveridge scheme was, in the event, paid for — by steadily increasing contribution rates accompanied by corresponding promises of increases in future benefits.

TABLE 1.1A
Social security budget: estimated expenditure at 1948/9 prices

| | Beveridge Report Estimates of cost | | |
	1945 (£m.)	1955 (£m.)	1965 (£m.)
Social insurance benefits			
Retirement pensions	142	214	339
Widow's and guardian's benefits	33	29	24
Unemployment benefit	124	123	121
Disability benefit	64	77	80
Industrial disability benefit	17	17	17
Maternity grant and benefit	8	7	7
Marriage grant	1	3	4
Funeral grant	5	8	14
Cost of administration	20	20	20
Total for social insurance benefits	414	498	626
National assistance			
Assistance pensions	44	37	28
Other assistance	6	6	6
Cost of administration	3	3	2
Total for national assistance	53	46	36
Children's allowances			
Allowances	124	122	112
Cost of administration	3	3	3
Total for children's allowances	127	125	115
Health services	192	192	192
Total expenditure	786	861	969

Sources:

(i) Beveridge Report estimates from *Social Insurance and Allied Services*, Cmdn. 6404, London, HMSO (1942), para. 58.

(ii) Actual cost taken from Ministry of Pensions, *Annual Reports*.

TABLE 1.1B
Social security budget: estimated expenditure at 1948/9 prices

Beveridge Report Actual cost		
1948/9 (£m.)	1955/6 (£m.)	1965/6 (£m.)
176.6	312.2	658.8
15.7	25.8	72.4
15.2	11.3	26.2
43.4 }	71.9 }	132.2 }
5.9	10.1	19.2
1	3	3
4	7	12
19.1	20.0	31.4
280.9	461.3	955.2
31.0 }	73.6 }	130.9 }
3	3	3
34.0	76.6	133.9
62.0	80.1	77.7
3	3	3
65.0	83.1	80.7
192	192	192
571.9	813.0	1361.8

*Beveridge assumed that the contribution made by the scheme to the health service would remain constant in real terms, and we have followed this in the 'actual cost' figures.

TABLE 1.2

Social security budget: estimated income at 1948/9 prices

	Beveridge report Estimates of finance needed						Actual results					
	1945 £m.	% of total	1955 £m.	% of total	1965 £m.	% of total	1948/9 £m.	% of total	1955/6 £m.	% of total	1965/6 £m.	% of total
Contributions from: Insured persons / Employers	374	48	374	43	366	38	286	50	412	51	785	58
Interest on existing funds	17	2	17	2	17	2	19	3	28	3	26	2
Balance of expenditure to be met from Exchequer (or local rates)	396	50	472	55	585	61	267	47	373	46	551	41
Total	787	100	863	100	968	100	572	100	813	100	1362	100

*Including, in 1945, payments from resources held by employers (or their insurers) for compensation on the old scales to persons injured before July 1944.

Sources: (i) Beveridge Report estimates derived from *Social Insurance and Allied Services*, para. 82.
(ii) Actual results derived from Ministry of Pensions, *Annual Reports*.

Tables 1.1 and 1.2 compare the outcomes with the plans. At the inception of the post-war national insurance schemes, expenditure was, at 1948/9 prices, some £200 million less than anticipated. The most important reason is that unemployment was well below the 8.5 per cent assumed in initial costings: the saving on unemployment benefit was over £100 million. Family allowances were less generous than Beveridge had proposed, and the cost of these was only half that allowed for in his costings.

The relationship between the general levels of national insurance benefits proposed by Beveridge and those actually implemented is a complex issue. Beveridge suggested that the basic rate of social insurance pension for a married couple would be £2 per week,[49] on the assumption that prices after the war would be some 25 per cent higher than in 1938.[50] Pensions would rise to this level from an initial £1.25.[51] It is clear that Beveridge underestimated the extent of wartime inflation, though less clear by how much. We estimate in Appendix C to this chapter that if Beveridge had undertaken in 1948 the calculation which led him to suggest a figure of £2, he would have proposed a benefit at that date of around £2.30 for a married couple. The basis of this estimate is discussed further in the following pages. The Government rejected Beveridge's proposed transitional period, and set benefits immediately at £2.10.[52] This was achieved for pensioners in 1946 and for all recipients of social benefits in 1948. It follows that pensions were almost 50 per cent higher than Beveridge had proposed, but other benefits around 10 per cent lower. Although this implied a higher overall level of benefits than the Beveridge Report had envisaged, the burden of this provision was reduced by the fact that wartime controls and subsidies had kept the rise in the subsistence cost of living significantly below the rise in the general price level. Financial problems initially seemed much less acute than anticipated, and by 1950 there was some euphoria about the achievements of the new system. The indefatigable Rowntree produced another study of poverty in York[53] which recorded only 3 per cent of the population in poverty, compared with 31 per cent from his 1936 study.

But the underlying problems remained. The Government Actuary[54] warned that this was simply a lull before the storm — his first quinquennial review of the post-war insurance scheme laid heavy stress on the magnitude of its unfunded liabilities. Little attention was paid at the time. The Government felt able to increase both benefit and contribution levels. By 1955 the total level of benefit expenditure was broadly in line with Beveridge's projections; the extra cost of retirement pensions was offset by the saving on unemployment benefit. The fund also gained from the implementation of the contribution increases, unrelated to benefit improvements, which had been planned from the inception of the scheme. The Exchequer share of total expenditure remained at its 1948/9 level.

The inevitable crisis broke quickly in the late 1950s. The number of pensioners continued to grow, and with it political concern for their welfare. The slogan 'You've never had it so good' illustrated the increases which had occurred in average earnings and the popular conception of subsistence income, and there was pressure to raise national insurance benefits in line. Demands on the National Insurance Fund increased, but the Government was not prepared to implement the required increase in general taxation. Its immediate response was the abandonment of any actuarial link between contributions and benefits. The Exchequer contribution was capped at a proportion of the current income of the National Insurance Fund, and contributions were to be levied at the rate necessary to match the current outflow from the fund, after Exchequer subsidy. The 'National Insurance Fund' was reduced to a piece of arcane book keeping. This move facilitated substantial increases in flat-rate national insurance contributions[55] but there was concern that taxation of this kind fell disproportionately on low-paid workers. Since contributions had now become a tax rather than a contribution for benefits to be received, the way was open to relate them to ability to pay and so an element of graduation by income was introduced. In return, the Government promised[56] graduated pensions – in future. It was the first step on the treadmill in which governments relieve their current financial pressure by raising money on the strength of still more generous benefits in future – a further step was to be taken in the 1970s with the introduction of the promise of comprehensive state earnings-related pensions.

By 1965, the end of Beveridge's proposed transitional period, the cost of social security as a whole was, in real terms, 25 per cent more than he had envisaged and the cost of retirement pensions twice as great. Beveridge had anticipated that about two-thirds of the expenditure would come from general taxation and one-third from national insurance contributions. The outcome was the other way round. General taxation provided little more than one-third of the cost, even though the role of the tax-financed national assistance was much greater than Beveridge had intended. Throughout the 1960s and 1970s, the level of national insurance contributions increased steadily. The increase was concentrated on the graduated component of the contribution, until by 1975 contributions were entirely earnings related. The budget of the National Insurance Fund was increased further when in the 1980s unemployment rose, for the first time, to levels at and above those envisaged in the Beveridge plan. In 1949, the first full year of the scheme, national insurance contributions were 5.5 per cent of the total wage and salary bill. In 1982 this figure was 16.3 per cent.

Social insurance and subsistence income

There was a second basic difficulty in the concept of social insurance against want. Social insurance relies on identifying in advance those contingencies which may cause hardship and building up protection against them through contributions. But the causes of poverty, and the public's conception of what it means by poverty, are likely to change over time. Can a scheme which bases current entitlement on past contributions be sufficiently adaptable to deal with differences in individual circumstances and changes in social conditions?

The fundamental nature of this problem is clear enough from the Beveridge Report itself. Beveridge argued that social insurance should provide benefits at levels related to subsistence income.[57] But there is an evident difficulty here. Subsistence income varies from household to household and from time to time. How can a benefit at one and the same time represent an actuarially fair return on past contributions and yet be set at the current subsistence needs of a particular family?

Beveridge wriggles on this hook but does not escape it. The problem is most obvious when he comes to consider the issue of rent. It is acknowledged that rent varies considerably across households for reasons that have little to do with the standard of housing which they enjoy.[58] It therefore follows that subsistence benefits should be related to the actual rent paid by the particular household. But to pay different amounts to different beneficiaries would clearly violate the contributory principle. Reluctantly but inevitably, Beveridge comes down in favour of including an average amount for rent in his levels of benefit. He expresses the – unfulfilled – hope that the problem of rent will be sorted out during the twenty-year transition.

The Government seized on this weakness to reject the principle that national insurance benefits should be related to subsistence income in any way. It is likely that this represented as much a desire to retain administrative flexibility and discretion as it did devotion to the strict logic of social insurance. But the principle that the level of national insurance benefits should be determined independently of the subsistence-based national assistance was established and, in the early days of the Beveridge scheme, it was the reality.

In 1948 the main national insurance benefits were paid to a married couple at the rate of £2.10 per week, while national assistance offered £2 plus rent.[59] It followed that any national insurance beneficiary with a rent of more than 10p per week, and without other resources, was entitled to national assistance. This was certainly not the relationship intended by Beveridge, who emphasised that national assistance should be distinctly less attractive than social insurance.[60] Wilson and Wilson[61] have commented that 'Cedric Sandford was reporting a widely accepted view when he wrote: "The explanation of the large and growing numbers of supplementary benefit claimants is very largely that the benefits were never set at the levels that Sir William had envisaged."' The suggestion that the scheme which the Liberal Beveridge devised for a predominantly Conservative Government failed because the post-war Labour Government was too mean to implement it is at first sight surprising. However, this conventional wisdom, which portrays the generous Sir William frustrated by a parsimonious government, does not appear to be supported by the facts.

It is not easy to decide exactly what Sir William had envisaged, since his suggested benefit rates were set in 1938 prices and raised by a notional 25 per cent to reflect wartime inflation. We can, however, attempt to reconstruct Beveridge's calculation in the light of post-war prices. This attempt is made in Appendix C to this chapter. The level of national insurance benefit for a married couple which this suggests Beveridge would have proposed at 1948 prices is between £2.15 and £2.39 per week, which may be compared with the actual benefit at that date of £2.10, without any reference to Beveridge's planned twenty-year transitional period. The level of national assistance, which Beveridge insisted should be distinctly less than the value of national insurance benefit, was at that date £2 per week, exclusive of rent; a reasonable allowance for rent might have been 55p. The relationship between social insurance and national assistance rates was distorted, not so much because insurance benefits were lower than intended, but because assistance rates were higher than intended.

As early as 1950, 25 per cent of all national insurance claimants also received national assistance.[62] National assistance rates were increased to reflect inflation but national insurance benefits were not, and the proportion obtaining both benefits rose to over 30 per cent. Beveridge himself pointed out[63] that this made nonsense of his scheme, as increasingly large numbers of households became eligible for national assistance. But it reflected the underlying logic of social insurance. Benefits were based on past contributions; national assistance rates were increased because governments wished to protect poor households against increases in the cost of living and give them some share of increasing national prosperity. Only when the link between benefits and contributions were eroded and finally abandoned (apart from the condition of having made some contributions), and national insurance pensions increased in ways which bore no relationship to contributions made, was the early relationship between national insurance and national assistance restored. This did no more than prevent any further increase in the proportion receiving both types of benefit. In the 1970s, pensions increased more rapidly than inflation,[64] but the supplementary benefit rate for the old was increased in line. The proportion of the old who received supplementary pensions fell as the other resources of pensioners increased. This was offset, however, by an increase[65] in the numbers of the unemployed and a fall in the real value of unemployment benefit as a result of incomplete indexation of

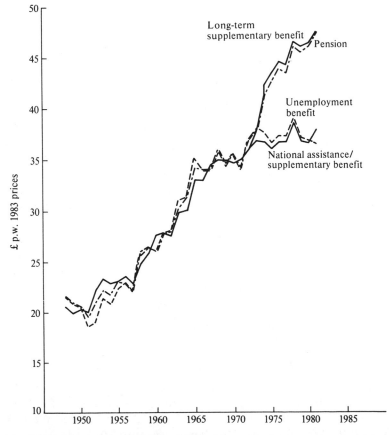

Fig. 1.2 Changing relative benefit levels: pension, national assistance/supplementary benefit, unemployment, at 1983 prices

benefit rates and the withdrawal of earnings-related supplements. Figure 1.2 shows the relative movements of benefit rates and Figure 1.3 the resulting effect on the numbers receiving national assistance or supplementary benefit. In 1982, one-third of national insurance beneficiaries also received supplementary benefits[66] − some 3 million claimants.

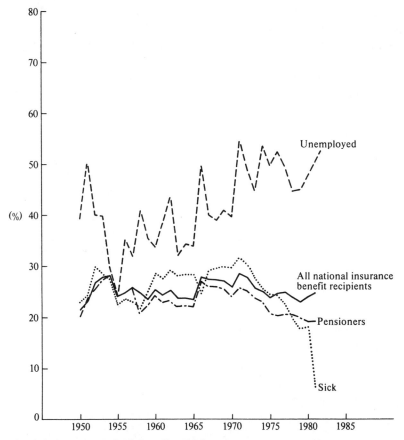

Fig. 1.3 Percentage of all benefit recipients dependent (in whole or part) on national assistance/supplementary benefit, 1950–1981

This historical account reveals the difficulty of achieving a rational relationship between a social insurance scheme and one of means-tested national assistance. If the contributory principle is to be taken seriously, then it is inconsistent with any fixed relationship between the two types of benefit. If, on the other hand, it is not to be taken seriously, then what is the justification for treating poor people who receive national insurance benefits differently from those who do not? And if there are to be separate schemes, then either the social insurance benefits must be very high, or the assistance benefits very low, or else – as has happened – large numbers of people will be involved in both.

Post-war developments

Social insurance is not a particularly flexible mechanism for the relief of poverty. It relies, for previously identified contingencies, on benefits which have been earned by past contributions. It follows that it can react only slowly to changing social or economic conditions. It is this feature which has led to the proliferation of *ad hoc* measures to deal with problems which Beveridge's plan for social security failed to foresee, and it is this, in turn, which has given rise to the complexity of the present system. We illustrate this by reference to two of the central issues in the post-war social security debate: the position of low-income working households and that of single-parent families.

The Beveridge Report barely discusses the problem of poverty among working households. In this, it is very much a product of the particular time at which it was written. Forty years before Beveridge, when Seebohm Rowntree undertook his first study of poverty in York (in 1896), he identified low earnings as the principal cause of poverty. Forty years after Beveridge, concern for the position of low-income households in work is evidenced in pressure both from the Left[67] who are concerned about family poverty – and from the Right,[68] who are exercised by the relationship between incomes in and out of work. But the Beveridge Report was written in the shadow of the Great Depression of the 1930s, and its principal theme is unemployment. Both the position of low-income working families and the position of the old receives much less attention. There is no hint of the political importance which provision for old age was to acquire in the post war era as the numbers of the elderly increased rapidly: the number of pensioner claimants grew between 1950 and 1970 from 4.2 million to 7.4 million.[69] For Beveridge it was axiomatic that anyone in employment had resources sufficient to support a wife and one child. Thus, so long as there were family allowances on an adequate scale for the second and subsequent children in a family, there could be no problem of the working poor.

In the twenty years after the Second World War, two things happened to alter this assessment. Although family allowances were introduced, their uprating attracted a low political priority. As Figure 1.4 shows, the total value of child support, including family allowances and child

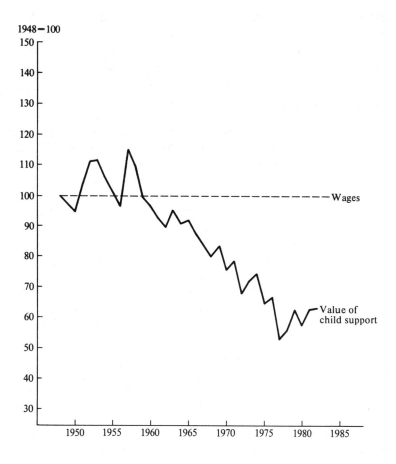

Fig. 1.4 The value of child support compared to wages: two-child-family, 1948–1982

tax allowances, failed to keep pace with rising wages. At the same time, increasing public expenditure overall raised direct taxes at all income levels, and the erosion of tax allowances relative to wages brought low-paid workers into the tax net in an unprecedented way. This trend was aggravated by the rising cost of social security itself, especially after the concept of national insurance contributions related to benefits was abandoned and they were raised to the levels needed to finance current outgoings.

In the mid-1960s, the Government came under considerable pressure to act to relieve family poverty. This issue was identified by Abel-Smith and Townsend[70] and pursued by the Child Poverty Action Group,[71] and attracted considerable political attention. Frightened by the cost of an increase in family allowances across the board, the Government implemented[72] a modest increase and accompanied it by a scheme of 'clawback', operated through the tax system, designed to recoup the increase from most taxpayers. Support for poor families was further increased by the introduction[73] of a specific means-tested family income supplement (FIS) in 1971.

Other policies also reflected this new concern. Local councils increasingly sought to protect poor households from the effect of general increases in rent levels, and rebate schemes became more extensive and more generous until a national scheme was introduced and extended to private-sector tenants. The Allen Committee[74] led to the introduction of a similar scheme of rate rebates, and this was greatly increased in scope in the mid-1970s. As health service charges were increased, governments came under pressure to exempt poor families and introduced various devices to achieve this result. In this way, means-tested benefits for poor working households proliferated outside the social insurance system and with rates and criteria unrelated to the operation of social insurance. By 1977 a widely quoted National Consumer Council survey discovered that there were forty-five different means tests in the social security system.[75]

The one-parent family was a contingency which Beveridge identified, worried about, but failed to deal with. Rather quaintly, from a modern perspective, he equated the position of the deserted wife with that of the victim of an industrial injury: both had lost their source of income through events connected with their occupation but for which they were not to be held responsible. Beveridge resisted, however, the logical conclusion of this analogy — that women in this position should be entitled to industrial injury benefit — and failed to propose any effective alternative solution.

Post-war social trends led to a substantial increase in the number of one-parent families, and this cause was one taken up by the family poverty lobby. The Finer Committee,[76] which reported in 1974, reflected official recognition of the issue. Although family income supplement was not exclusively directed at one-parent families, a high proportion of recipients[77] do in fact fall into this category. A number of specific provisions were also introduced — a premium on child benefit,[78] an enhanced tax allowance,[79] and a specially favourable basis for supplementary benefit entitlement.[80] The capricious relationship between gross and net incomes which these uncoordinated benefits imply is illustrated in Chapter 4.

Social insurance relies for its effectiveness on successfully identifying in advance the potential causes of poverty. But it was absurd to suppose that Beveridge in 1942 could successfully have anticipated the changing social and economic needs of the post-war world, and in fact for the next forty years his concern for the problem of unemployment was to prove greatly exaggerated. In consequence, his design has required endless buttressing with *ad hoc* expedients which have taken us far away from the social insurance principle.

The State Earnings-Related Pension Scheme

The most important single explicit reform to the Beveridge social security plan was the introduction, from 1978, of the State Earnings Related Pension Scheme (SERPS).[81] Under it, retirement pensioners will receive an earnings-related pension in addition to their basic state pension. This pension is based on qualifying earnings — in 1983/4 those of between £32.50 and £235 per week. The best twenty years of qualifying earnings are revalued to the date of retirement in line with national average earnings, and the earnings-related pension is one-quarter of the resulting average. Since it is only income after 1978 that can be considered as qualifying earnings, this scheme will not approach maturity until after 1998. When fully operative, it will cost an additional £10-£15 billion at 1982 prices,[82] thus increasing the overall social security budget by around one-third, equivalent to approximately ten points on the basic rate of income tax or to an addition of about the same figure to the standard national insurance contribution rate.

There is provision for good occupational pension schemes to be 'contracted out' of SERPS.[83] The phrase 'contracting out' is something of a misnomer, since contracted-out employees will still in due course receive an earnings-related state pension like anyone else. But a contracted-out scheme must promise to provide at least a 'guaranteed minimum pension', calculated accordingly to a similarly complex but somewhat different formula from that used to compute earnings-related pensions, and the earnings-related state pension will be reduced by a corresponding amount. In return, employers and employees who participate in contracted-out schemes pay lower rates of national insurance contributions on current qualifying earnings. The reduction is currently slightly over 2 per cent for employees and 4 per cent for employers. Contracting out is best seen as a device by which the state lends money, on fairly 'soft' terms, to occupational (including public sector) pension schemes.

An explanation of the design of the scheme requires some understanding of its political history. At the 1959 election, the Labour Party proposed an extensive scheme of 'national superannuation'.[84] There were several different motives. The power of the growing pensioner population as a new and major political interest group had been widely recognised by both major political parties in the 1950s. The Left was concerned by the political and economic consequences of growth in the resources of the occupational pension sector. A division between middle-class employees – who were generally eligible for private pensions – and manual workers – who relied on state provision – was increasingly evident.

Although the Labour Party lost the 1959 election, the principal architect of its national superannuation proposals, Richard Crossman, remained strongly committed to them. When Crossman became Secretary of State for Health and Social Security in 1968, the development of 'national superannuation' became an early priority. Although controversial,[85] Crossman's proposals gained Parliamentary approval[86] and, but for Labour's defeat in the 1970 general election, would have come into effect.

The new Conservative Government introduced alternative proposals[87] of its own. These gave the dominant role in the extension of pension provision to the private sector and supplemented it with a 'state reserve scheme'. The state reserve scheme was to be a government-run, funded scheme, modelled on private occupational schemes but clearly and intentionally inferior to any but the poorest of them. These measures also reached the statute book,[88] and also died when the government which had sponsored them was defeated at the polls.

It was recognised by all sides that a continuation of this political see-saw was intolerable, and that any new proposals should command bipartisan support. SERPS[89] is the product of extensive negotiations between the various interest groups, and its main elements went through Parliament without significant opposition. It represented a truce which allowed existing occupational pension schemes to continue in operation without any substantial modification of their current activities, while giving the major role in extending pension provision for other workers to the state. But the primary objective in devising SERPS was not to find the best pension scheme for the early twenty-first century, but to construct proposals to which all parties might agree. This is evident in the complexity of the scheme, and in its weaknesses, which we discuss further in Chapter 2.

The contributory principle

The Beveridge Report took the concept of insurance extremely seriously. Contributions were to be levied on an actuarially calculated basis to reflect the benefits received. Surpluses were to be invested to provide against future claims.

The retreat from this principle has been comprehensive. The concept of funding future benefits — which means the pain comes now and the pleasure later — is profoundly unattractive to politicians, and was the part of the Beveridge plan to be most immediately rejected. However, in introducing full-rate pensions straight away, the Government acknowledged a funding deficiency to be met from general taxation. When the time came to pay the subsidy on any substantial scale, the pledge was abandoned and a 'pay as you go' basis adopted. The National Insurance Fund was reduced to meaningless accounting and the actuarial link between contributions and benefits abandoned. It is clear that the present national insurance scheme is not a contributory one in the sense intended by the Beveridge Report. Nevertheless 'contribution records' continue to be maintained, at an annual cost of around £100 million, and those concerned with social security continue to talk about the 'contributory principle'. It is difficult to define exactly what the contributory principle is. In Appendix A to this chapter we reproduce the 'six fundamental principles' of the Beveridge Report, and in Appendix B we present the most recent public attempt by a DHSS official to explain to Parliament the significance of the contributory principle.

There are a number of forms a relationship between the state and the individual might take. First, it could be a purely commercial arrangement, such as that which exists between insurance companies and their customers. Payments by individuals would then be reflected in actuarially calculated benefits from the scheme. It was certainly this sort of relationship that Beveridge had in mind, although even the original proposals required the state to make additional contributions. A second possible form is that of the compulsory club where subscriptions and benefits are unrelated, but membership of the club is necessary before any benefit is paid. Finally, the loosest relationship would have contributions entirely dedicated to the provision of benefits but with the allocation of benefits left to the state, and benefits can be paid to those who have made no contribution at all.

In fact, the national insurance scheme as it has developed exhibits features of all three forms, but in a rather incoherent manner. The original proponents of social insurance saw in it a contractual relationship between the state and individuals, in which the Government would perceive an obligation to specify benefits and in due course to provide them. But governments have increased[90] and reduced[91] the real value of pensions in payment; brought in earnings-related supplements to benefit[92] and withdrawn them;[93] changed uprating formulae frequently and arbitrarily;[94] and altered the level and the tax status[95] of benefits and contributions. In all the debate on these issues, arguments based on the contractual nature of past benefit promises have played the most minor of roles. The principal assurance that pension promises will be honoured is provided, not by a mutually understood contractual relationship between the individual and the state, but by the political power of pensioners as an interest group. It is in response to this political power that the so-called 'insurance' benefit given to pensioners has steadily increased in relation to the so-called 'insurance' benefit given to the unemployed. It is a reflection of the significance attached to the insurance principle that the argument 'You cannot cut my un-employment benefit because I've paid for it' is hardly thought worth using.

National insurance contributions began as a payment related to one's own prospective benefits. They became a levy based on the current benefits given to others. In 1977, the Government imposed[96] a surcharge on the employer's contribution, for general revenue purposes. In 1981 and 1982 it increased employee contributions[97] for precisely the same reason. The level of national insurance contributions, like any other tax, is now set by the overall revenue needs of the Government.

Beveridge envisaged that people would·be more willing to pay national insurance contributions than other taxes because they would approve of the purpose. There is no evidence that individuals distinguish carefully the nature of the various deductions from their pay. But taxes which raise revenue for a specific purpose do have the merit of increasing public perception of the links between Government revenue and expenditure. Some items of social security expenditure, particularly pensions, are popular, and many countries use an earmarked social security tax for this reason. Perhaps we should do the same.

However social security expenditure is financed, it may be necessary to impose some conditions for qualification for receipt of benefits. At present, anyone who is resident in the UK is entitled to most social security benefits. The principal restriction on the payment of such benefits to the poor of the world is the use of immigration procedures to prevent entry by those who are not UK citizens and who are likely to resort to the social security system if admitted. Although some-what arbitrary, these procedures do not appear to cause great practical difficulties in implementation, and similar ones exist, and are thought necessary, in other Western countries.

For national insurance benefits, there is a series of rather complicated tests based on contribution records (either in the UK or in another member state of the EEC). But if national insurance contributions are, as they must be, seen as a tax on income rather than an actuarially calculated payment for prospective benefits, it is hard to see any justification for this. Why should someone who has paid more in national insurance contributions over a forty-year span obtain a lower pension than someone who has paid less over a fifty-year span? If the answer is that the pension should be related to the length of a working life, then the corollary is that it is that, and not a national insurance contribution record, that should determine pension entitlement.

There is really nothing left of the contributory principle in national insurance but 10,000 civil servants administering contribution records, and a good deal of intellectual lumber. It is time to consider whether we need either.

Conclusion

Despite its evident practical failure, the concept of social insurance continues to have a wide-ranging appeal. There are those on the Right who are reluctant to accept explicitly that the state should become involved in determining the distribution and redistribution of income, but are also reluctant to accept the social and political consequences of its failing to do so. Social insurance appears to reconcile these positions. There are those on the Left who see the notion of social insurance as one which entrenches redistribution to the poor as an entitlement rather than something dependent on a political process and, ultimately, on the consent of those who give up the resources which make it possible. But both these arguments are based on illusion, as practical experience has demonstrated. Social insurance implies that individuals make contributions and dispositions which they would not make voluntarily, otherwise it would not be necessary for the state to impose it. It follows that redistribution is an essential part of social insurance, and we ought to recognise that and agree on what kind of redistribution it is that we want. It also follows that the nature and extent of such redistribution will inevitably depend on the political attitudes of the day. Social insurance is not insurance, but it is inescapably social.

Appendix A: The fundamental principles of the Beveridge plan

Beveridge listed six 'fundamental principles' of his plan for social security. They were:

304. *Flat Rate of Subsistence Benefit*: The first fundamental principle of the social insurance scheme is provision of a flat rate of insurance benefit, irrespective of the amount of the earnings which have been interrupted by unemployment or disability or ended by retirement; exception is made only where prolonged disability has resulted from an industrial accident or disease. This principle follows from the recognition of the place and importance of voluntary insurance in social security and distinguishes the scheme proposed for Britain from the security schemes of Germany, the Soviet Union, the United States and most other countries with the exception of New Zealand. The flat rate is the same for all the principal forms of cessation of earning – unemployment, disability, retirement; for maternity and for widowhood there is a temporary benefit at a higher rate.

The Beveridge proposal that benefits should be related to subsistence needs was rejected immediately by the Government. In 1961 graduated pensions were introduced and in 1966 earnings-related supplements to sickness and unemployment benefit. The former was terminated in 1975 and the latter in 1982. Since 1978, however, a new scheme of earnings-related pension has operated. The Beveridge principle that the flat rate should be the same for all forms of cessation of earnings was initially accepted but eventually abandoned in favour of an (increasingly large) differential in favour of pensioners.

305. *Flat Rate of Contribution*: The second fundamental principle of the scheme is that the compulsory contribution required of each insured person or his employer is at a flat rate, irrespective of his means. All insured persons, rich or poor, will pay the same contributions for the same security; those with larger means will pay more only to the extent that as tax-payers they pay more to the National Exchequer and so to the State share of the Social Insurance Fund. This feature distinguishes the scheme proposed for Britain from the scheme recently established in New Zealand under which the contributions are graduated by income, and are in effect an income-tax assigned to a particular service. Subject moreover to one exception, the contribution will be the same irrespective of the assumed degree of risk affecting particular individuals or forms of employment. The exception is the raising of a proportion of the special cost of benefits and pensions for industrial disability in occupations of high risk by a levy on employers proportionate to risk and pay-roll (paras. 86–90 and 360).

Graduated contributions were introduced in 1961. Since 1975 contributions have been entirely earnings related.

306. *Unification of Administrative Responsibility*: The third fundamental principle is unification of administrative responsibility in the interests of efficiency and economy. For each insured person there will be a single weekly contribution, in respect of all his benefits. There will be in each locality a Security Office able to deal with claims of every kind and all sides of security. The methods of paying different kinds of cash benefit will be different and will take account of the circumstances of insured persons, providing for payment at the home or elsewhere, as is necessary. All contributions will be paid into a single Social Insurance Fund and all benefits and other insurance payments will be paid from that fund.

Surprisingly, this is perhaps the one of Beveridge's principles closest to being achieved. Since the Department of Employment's role in payment of unemployment benefit has been reduced, administrative responsibility for most benefits falls on only two authorities – the DHSS and the local authority.

307. *Adequacy of Benefit*: The fourth fundamental principle is adequacy of benefit in amount and in time. The flat rate of benefit proposed is intended in itself to be sufficient without further resources to provide the minimum income needed for subsistence in all normal cases. It gives room and a basis for additional voluntary provision, but does not assume that in any case. The benefits are adequate also in time, that is to say except for contingencies of a temporary nature, they will continue indefinitely without means test, so long as the need continues, though subject to any change of conditions and treatment required by prolongation of the interruption in earning and occupation.

The flat rate of benefit has at no time been sufficient to provide resources equal to the supplementary benefit level in the normal case. On 13 November 1980, for example, 825,000 (51 per cent) of the 1,604,000 unemployed were in receipt of supplementary benefit.[98]

308. *Comprehensiveness*: The fifth fundamental principle is that social insurance should be comprehensive, in respect both of the persons covered and of their needs. It should not leave either to national assistance or to voluntary insurance any risk so general or so uniform that social insurance can be justified. For national assistance involves a means test which may discourage voluntary insurance or personal saving. And voluntary insurance can never be sure of covering the ground. For any need moreover which, like direct funeral expenses, is so general and so uniform as to be a fit subject for insurance by compulsion, social insurance is much cheaper to administer than voluntary insurance.

In 1983/4, 4 million people were in receipt of supplementary benefit or supplementary pensions.[99]

309. *Classification*: The sixth fundamental principle is that social insurance, while unified and comprehensive, must take account of the different ways of life of different sections of the community; of those dependent on earnings by employment under contract of service, of those earning in other ways, of those rendering vital unpaid service as housewives, of those not yet of age to earn and of those past earning. The term 'classification' is used here to denote adjustment of insurance to the differing circumstances of each of these classes and to many varieties of need and circumstance within each insurance class. But the insurance classes are not economic or social classes in the ordinary sense; the insurance scheme is one for all citizens irrespective of their means.

Of the six principles, this one is the most difficult to assess, or to define. We have argued above that it was the inability of insurance to adjust to differing circumstances which proved to be a principal cause of its failure.

Appendix B: The DHSS and the contributory principle

Extract from *Minutes of Evidence*, Subcommittee of the House of Commons Treasury and Civil Service Committee, Session 1982-3, 'The Structure of Personal Income Taxation and Income Support', paras. 838-41.

[Mr Wainwright]

838. As to the benefits, could we explore the rationale nowadays, bearing in mind all the other non-contributory benefits which are available, of the contribution record system?

(*Mr Regan*) I think there are two points, and I am not sure which one you are after. If you are asking whether there is a rationale for a contribution record, I think the answer is simply that if you did not have a contribution record as a basis for entitlement to benefit you would have to have some other test. I do not think you would simply be able to accept that anybody, including anybody who had just arrived in the country, who had made no contributions should get a retirement pension or short-term benefit, so you have to have some test, and it seems to us probable that the contribution test is as good a one as any. Otherwise people like married women and widows who have opted out of National Insurance contributions would be eligible for benefits without any test at all and you would have a very large increase in benefit expenditure. I am not sure whether you were directing your remarks to the question whether there was a justification for a contributory principle?

839. Yes, and also what justification there is for the particular contribution requirement which to my mind bears very little relationship to the benefits received. It seems to be an extraordinarily arbitrary system because in no way is a certain level of contribution paid for an average benefit.

(*Mr Regan*) I think one could certainly accept it as true that there are very easy tests for short-term benefits–though not for benefits where a lifetime average has to be maintained. There is a certain justification for this in the relative ease administratively with which it is done now that these records are computerised. If the computers are working all right we can do it easily and do not have to go to employers. You have a record on the basis of which short-term benefits are calculated. Whether it is too easy a test is a matter of judgment. One issue which enters into it is the question whether, if you made it more difficult, you would have to pay out more in supplementary benefit, if entitlement to supplementary benefit was increased. That is probably in itself not a desirable thing to do. On the question of the contributory principle, I am a National Insurance man born and bred and for over 30 years I have firmly believed that it is a principle which is worth maintaining and has a rationale in its acceptance even now despite all that has happened. You have quoted non-contributory benefits. The great majority of our fellow citizens believe there is a direct relationship between what they pay and what eventually they get out of it at the end of the day as of right without the proof required for means-tested benefits, and that is something which people value.

Mr Howell

840. Do you agree that that is mumbo-jumbo?

(*Mr Regan*) I can only give you my view, which I have just expressed.

Mr Howell: It sounds like mumbo-jumbo to me.

Mr Wainwright

841: You have not answered the second part of my question. How on earth are the contribution requirements fixed and what relationship to they bear to the marvellous benefits they unlock?

(*Mr Regan*) They are not fixed on any particularly rational basis but on the basis that you want a reasonable test and do not want to make it too hard for people to get the benefits, because, after all, the contingencies are there and you do not want resort to means-tested benefits. But all the benefits in some sense are based on a pay as you go system, which is what the National Insurance system is. If you like, all the benefits are too easy. None of us has ever paid, or will ever pay, because even on the pension side it is not actuarially calculated, the full value of our benefits. This is a function of the inter-generation apportionment process whereby the working generation today basically pays for the pensions of the generation which has now retired and we go forward in the hope that each successive generation will, in return for something which is much less than full value, go on doing so. I do not think there is a particular sort of logic to any particular figure.

Mr. C.M. Regan is an Under Secretary in the Family Support and Supplementary Benefit Division of the DHSS.

Appendix C: Beveridge's subsistence level

Beveridge considered carefully[100] the minimum levels of income his scheme needed to satisfy. Evidence on minimum requirements was gleaned from a number of sources, and his suggested 'minimum' for a non-pensioner couple with no children, at 1938 prices, was as follows:

	Shillings per week
Food	13s.
Clothing	3s.
Fuel, light, and sundries	4s.
Margin	2s.
Rent	10s.
Total	32s.

The Beveridge Report cites the 1936 and 1938 reports of the Technical Commission on Nutrition of the League of Nations and the 1933 Committee on Nutrition of the British Medical Association as providing a basis for 13s. per week as capable of providing an adequate diet. Clothing was set at 3s., below the level implied by Ministry of Labour family budgets, on the grounds that 'in none of the Social Surveys undertaken in various towns before the war was the cost of clothing for a man and a woman put as high as 3/-' and that 'clothing is an item of expenditure that can for a time be postponed' (para. 219). Fuel expenditure was set at an average level for the lowest quartile of households and a small amount (5d.) added for other costs. A margin was allowed 'for inefficiency in purchasing'. The report recognises the large variability of rent payments and expresses the hope that this will improve, recognising that: 'No scale of Social Insurance benefits free from objection can be framed while the failure continues' (para. 216). The (uniform) 10s. per household included in the subsistence level is defended by citing a survey of rents paid by applicants for war service grants, and Rowntree's 1936 study of incomes in York.[101]

Beveridge also worked out a subsistence level for pensioners. Their

TABLE 1.3
Price indices 1938-1948 compared

	Board of Trade Cost of Living Index and Interim Index	Seers's Working-Class Index* (March (1948)	Feinstein†
	(1948 with 1938 = 100)		
All items	141	172	189
Food	123	150	159
Clothing	181	182	210
Fuel and light	174	158	153
Other goods	n/a	167	191
Rent and rates	109	110	–
Housing	–	–	126

* D. Seers, *Changes in the Cost of Living and the Distribution of Income since 1938*, Oxford, Blackwell (1949).
† C. H. Feinstein, *Statistical Tables of National Income, Expenditure and Output 1855-1956*, Cambridge (1976), Table 62 (Consumer Goods and Services).

food requirements were, he decided, some 1*s*. 6*d*. per week below those of non-pensioners, their clothing 4*d*. below and their rent 1*s*. 6*d*. below, but their increased heating needs meant that he allowed an extra 1*s*. for fuel. Overall, his subsistence level per week for a pensioner couple was 29*s*. 8*d*., 2*s*. 4*d*. below their non-pensioner counterparts. Despite this calculation, the post-war level of benefit was to be 40*s*. per week (the same as the non-pensioner subsistence level, with an assumed 25 per cent price rise between 1938 and implementation) for both the unemployed and for pensioners, although for pensioners this would only be achieved after a twenty-year transitional period.

Deciding what would have been the appropriate level of benefit required to implement in 1948 the subsistence level of income Beveridge intended is a hazardous exercise. Official price indices of the time are now regarded, in the words of Cole,[102] as 'seriously misleading', in part because of their failure to take account of changes in the pattern of expenditures. Seers reweighted the series to produce a Working-Class Index in 1949.[103] Table 1.3 compares evidence on price movements between 1938 and 1948 of various items in the pre-1947 Cost of Living Index, linked to the post-1947 Interim Index of Retail Prices, with the Seers recalculation, and with a more recent compilation by Feinstein and others.[104] The Feinstein series gives considerably higher price rises for all items except fuel.

Using the three sets of price indices gives different indications of the required level to satisfy the subsistence level Beveridge intended. Table 1.4 shows that, for a non-pensioner married couple, the 'official' indices would imply a requirement of 42*s*. 1*d*. per week, and with the Seers adjustments, of 45*s*. 8*d*., while the Feinstein indices would imply

TABLE 1.4
Beveridge's subsistence levels at 1948 prices
(s. and d. per week)

	Using official indices	Using Seers	Using Feinstein
Food*	16s. 1d.	19s. 6d.	20s. 8d.
Clothing†	5s. 5d.	5s. 5d.	6s. 3d.
Fuel, light, and sundries‡	6s. 11d.	6s. 4d.	6s. 1d.
Margin §	2s. 10d.	3s. 5d.	3s. 9d.
Rent¶	10s. 10d.	11s.	11s. ¶
Total	42s. 1d.	45s. 8d.	47s. 9d.

Notes: Deflated by: *food index; †clothing; ‡ fuel and light; § all items; ¶ rent and rates, and ¶ rent taken from Seers.
Sources: As Table 1.3.

47s. 9d. None of these figures are very far above the level at which benefits actually were set.

The Beveridge Report was published shortly after the publication of the results of Rowntree's study of York in 1936 and the national insurance scheme was implemented three years before Rowntree and Lavers's 1950 study.[105] Both of these studies also attempted to set minimum levels of subsistence income. The 1936 Rowntree study set a 'poverty line' *without rent* of 27s. 8d. per week for an unemployed couple in 1936 prices compared with Beveridge's 22s. in 1938 prices. Table 1.5 compares the three subsistence levels at 1948 prices using the official and Feinstein's sets of price indices.

The striking feature of the table is just how much less generous the Beveridge subsistence level was than either of the Rowntree studies in setting its minimum level. On either price basis, the Beveridge 'poverty line' was only around two-thirds of that of Rowntree's. Beveridge's allowance for food was a little below that of either Rowntree's study, and his allowance for clothing was between a half and two-thirds. However, the main difference was that, apart from the 'margin' allowed for inefficiency in purchasing, the Beveridge line contained no allowance for expenditure other than food, clothing or fuel, while both Rowntree studies allowed for household and personal expenditure on such items as writing paper, stamps, newspaper, wireless, trade union subscription, tobacco, and beer, etc.

TABLE 1.5
Beveridge's subsistence income compared to Rowntree's
(1948 prices throughout, s. and d. per week)

Using official indices	Beveridge 1938	Rowntree 1936†	Rowntree and Lavers 1950§
Food	16s. 1d.	17s. 5d.	21s. 9d.
Clothing	5s. 5d.	10s. 5d.	9s. 9d.
Fuel and light	6s.11d.	5s.11d.	6s. 6d.
Household sundries	–	1s. 6d.	5s. 5d.
Margin	2s.10d.	–	–
Personal and other	–	8s.	8s. 6d.
Total before rent	31s. 3d.	43s. 3d.	51s.11d.
Rent	10s.10d.		
Total after rent	42s. 1d.		

Using Feinstein¶			
Food	20s.8d.	22s.5d.	20s. 9d.
Clothing	6s.3d.	12s.	10s. 9d.
Fuel and light	6s.1d.	5s.2d.	7s. 2d.
Household sundries	–	2s.1d.	5s.11d.
Margin	3s.9d.	–	–
Personal and other	–	10s.9d.	8s. 9d.
Total before rent	36s.9d.	52s.5d.	53s. 4d.
Rent	11s.		
Total after rent	47s.9d.		

* *Social Insurance and Allied Services.*
† B. S. Rowntree, *Poverty and Progress: A Second Social Survey of York,* London, New York, and Toronto, Longman Green (1941).
§ B. S. Rowntree and G. R. Lavers, *Poverty and the Welfare State,* London, New York, and Toronto, Longman Green (1951).
¶ *Statistical Tables of National Income, Expenditure and Output, 1855–56.*

References and notes

1. *The Poor Law Report of 1834* ed. S.G. Checkland and E.O.A. Checkland, Harmondsworth, Penguin (1974).
2. Poor Law Amendment Act 1834. This was added to by the Poor Law Outdoor Relief Regulation Order (1852) which allowed for a 'labour test' after which outdoor relief was granted. Poor Law relief outside the workhouse was consolidated in the Relief Regulation Order (1911).
3. For a discussion, see A.I. Ogus, 'Great Britain', in P.H. Kohler and H.F. Zacher (eds.), *The Evolution of Social Insurance,* London, Frances Pinter (1982), p. 157 et seq.

4. Checkland and Checkland, op. cit., pp. 114–16 and p. 334.
5. In the National Assistance Act 1948. The Unemployment Act of 1934 paved the way for an Unemployment Assistance Board (1935) which replaced the Poor Law administration for the unemployed. This in turn became the Assistance Board, and then the National Assistance Board from 1948.
6. Booth's findings were published in two articles in the *Journal of the Royal Statistical Society*: 'The Inhabitants of Tower Hamlets . . .' (50, p. 326) and 'The Conditions and Occupations of the People of East London and Hackney 1887' (51, p. 276). The general inquiry was published in seventeen volumes entitled *The Life and Labour of the People in London* (London, Macmillan, 1902–4).
7. B.S. Rowntree, *Poverty: A Study of Town Life*, London, Macmillan (1902).
8. See M.E. Rose, *The Relief of Poverty: 1834–1914*, London, Macmillan (1972). In the early 1840s about 20 per cent of able-bodied persons in receipt of Poor Law relief were being aided because of insufficient wages (see Rose, 'The Allowance System under the New Poor Law', *Historical Review*, 19, Ec.608) and the rate of pauperism tended to be highest where casual labour predominated. The main cause of poverty in Rowntree's 1902 study was also low wages.
9. See P.H.J.H. Gosden, *Self-Help: Voluntary Associations in Nineteenth-Century Britain*, London, Batsford (1974).
10. See J. Harris, *Unemployment and Politics*, Oxford University Press (1972). See also B. Gilbert, *The Evolution of National Insurance in Great Britain*, London, Michael Joseph (1966).
11. See D. Fraser, *The Evolution of the British Welfare State*, London, Macmillan (1973).
12. Fraser, op. cit., p. 115.
13. W.L. Blackley, 'National Insurance: A Cheap, Practical and Regular Means of Abolishing Poor Rates', *Nineteenth Century*, 4, 834–57.
14. *Report of the Select Committee on National Provident Insurance*, H.C. 257 (1887).
15. The Bismarckian legislation of 1881–3 is discussed in, among others, W.H. Dawson, *Bismarck and State Socialism*, London, Frome (1890); B.W. Wells, 'Compulsory Insurance in Germany' (1891), reprinted in *Political Science, 2* (June 1935); Dawson, *Social Insurance in Germany*, London, Tonbridge Press (1912); and A. Ashley, *The Social Policy of Bismarck*, London (1912).
16. See Ogus, op. cit., p. 171 et seq.
17. *Report of the Royal Commission on the Aged Poor*, Cmnd. 7684 (1895). The argument was that as the number of aged poor was declining, a pension scheme was unnecessary.
18. See F.H. Stead, *How Old Age Pensions Began to Be*, London (1910).
19. A talk given in London in 1898 by the Agent-General of New Zealand was used by Booth to launch the British campaign. See Ogus, op. cit., pp. 172–3.
20. *Report of the Departmental Committee on Old Age Pensions* Cmnd. 8911 (1898). Joseph Chamberlain exerted considerable pressure for the establishment of this committee – see Ogus, op. cit., p. 178.
21. This was set up under the influence of a pamphlet published by Charles Booth arguing for a universal old-age pension (*Old Age Pensions and the Aged Poor*, London, Macmillan, 1889), and for the next nine years sponsored a programme for the introduction of a universal scheme until the Old-Age Pensions Act 1908. See Gilbert, op. cit., p. 193 et seq.
22. *Report of the Select Committee on the Aged Deserving Poor*, H.C. 296 (1899).
23. P. Thane, 'Non-contributory Versus Insurance Pensions, 1878–1908', in Thane (ed.), *The Origins of British Social Policy*, (1978), especially p. 98.

The new national scheme was implemented in the Old-Age Pensions Act 1908. Pensions, financed from general taxation, were payable to persons aged 70 and above, whose means did not exceed a certain amount.

24. Thane, op. cit., pp. 113-15.
25. The last act of the outgoing Conservative Government in 1905 was to set up the Royal Commission on the Poor Law, reflecting a belief that all that was needed was a more efficient poor-law system combined with other measures on old age and unemployment. The incoming Liberal administration had other ideas; there is some controversy over whether this was forced on them or reflected a conscious reaction to changing attitudes to social welfare. See J. Hay, *The Origins of the Liberal Social Welfare Reforms: 1906-1914*, London (1975).
26. National Insurance Act 1911. Part I established the health scheme with compulsory insurance for most manual workers between 16 and 70, and for other employed persons earning less than a prescribed amount.
27. See Ogus, op. cit., pp. 184-5, for a discussion.
28. The new scheme was confined to industries with seasonal fluctuations; shipbuilding, engineering, construction, etc., and thus omitted those with a relatively stable employment record (for whom the need was less pressing) and those where unemployment was more chronic (and therefore difficult to handle). See B. Gilbert, *British Social Policy 1914-1939*, London, Batsford (1970), p. 53.
29. See Ogus, op. cit., p. 187 and p. 205.
30. See C.L. Mowat, *Britain between the Wars: 1918-1940*, London, Methuen (1955), for a discussion.
31. A. Ogus and E. Barendt, *Law of Social Security*, London, Butterworth (1978).
32. Report by Sir William Beveridge, *Social Insurance and Allied Services*, Cmnd. 6404, London, HMSO (1942).
33. House of Commons, 16 February 1943, col. 16/8.
34. *Social Insurance Part I* (White Paper), Cmnd. 6550, and *Social Insurance Part II, Workmen's Compensation* (White Paper), Cmnd. 6551, London, HMSO (1944).
35. Beveridge, op. cit., p. 6 and p. 17.
36. The debate on *Social Insurance and Allied Services* took place in the House of Commons between 16 February and 18 February 1943.
37. J. Harris, *William Beveridge*, Oxford University Press (1977), p. 473.
38. Ibid.
39. For details, see 'Memorandum by the Government Actuary', Appendix A in Beveridge, op. cit., p. 175 et seq.
40. Beveridge, op. cit., para. 448, p. 167.
41. This is made explicit in the report. Beveridge (op. cit., paras. 217-32, pp. 84-90) is concerned with setting the levels of benefits required to provide a subsistence income.
42. For a discussion see V. George, *Social Security: Beveridge and After*, London, Routledge and Kegan Paul (1968), p. 51 et seq.
43. National Insurance Act 1948.
44. Gilbert, *British Social Policy 1914-1939*, op. cit.
45. 'Memorandum by the Government Actuary', Appendix A in Beveridge, op. cit., para. 5, pp. 175-7.
46. National Insurance Act 1971.
47. Gilbert, *British Social Policy 1914-1939*, op. cit., para. 13, p. 180.
48. Ibid., paras. 77-82.
49. Beveridge, op. cit., para. 401, p. 150.
50. 'Memorandum by the Government Actuary', Appendix A in Beveridge, op. cit., para. 4, p. 174.

51. Ibid., para. 5, p. 175.
52. National Insurance Act 1946.
53. B.S. Rowntree and G.R. Lavers, *Poverty and the Welfare State*, London, New York, and Toronto, Longman Green (1951).
54. *Report by the Government Actuary on the First Quinquennial Review*, London, HMSO (1955).
55. The flat rate of NI contributions was increased, in 1948 prices, from £0.144 in 1948, to £0.135 in 1952, and to £0.166 in 1958 (*Social Security Statistics 1973*, and *Economic Trends*, Annual Supplement 1983, London, HMSO).
56. *Provision for Old Age*, Cmnd. 638, London, HMSO (1958).
57. Beveridge, op. cit., para. 193, p. 76.
58. Ibid., para. 197, p. 77.
59. National Assistance Act 1948.
60. Beveridge, op. cit., para. 369, p. 141.
61. T. Wilson and D.J. Wilson, *The Political Economy of the Welfare State*, London, Allen and Unwin (1982).
62. Ministry of Pensions, *Annual Report 1950*, London, HMSO.
63. Harris, *William Beveridge*, op. cit.
64. In 1982 prices, the married-couple pension rose from £37.80 per week in 1970 to £48.30 in 1980 (*Social Security Statistics 1972* and *1981*, London, HMSO).
65. In 1970, there were 596,000 registered unemployed, of whom 203,000 (34 per cent) were dependent on supplementary benefit. By 1980 this had risen to 1,895,000, with 825,000 (43.5 per cent) dependent on supplementary benefit (*Social Security Statistics 1972* and *1981*).
66. *The Government's Expenditure plans 1982-3 to 1985-6*, London, HMSO Cmnd. 8789, London, HMSO, Tables 2.12.3 and 2.12.4.
67. The main proponents of higher benefit levels for those in work are the Child Poverty Action Group and the Low Pay Unit.
68. See, for example, A.P.L. Minford, *Unemployment: Cause and Cure*, Oxford, Martin Robertson (1982) and H. Parker, *The Moral Hazard of Social Security Benefits*, London, IEA (1983).
69. Ministry of Pensions and National Insurance, *Annual Report 1958*, London, HMSO.
70. B. Abel-Smith and P. Townsend, *The Poor and the Poorest*, London, G. Bell (1965).
71. CPAG was founded in 1965. See F. Field, 'A Pressure Group for the Poor', in D. Bull (ed.), *Family Poverty*, London, Duckworth (1972).
72. Finance Act 1968.
73. Family Income Supplements Act 1970.
74. *Report of the Committee of Enquiry on the Impact of Rates on Households*, Cmnd. 2582, London, HMSO (1965).
75. National Consumer Council, *Means Tested Benefits*, London, NCC (1977).
76. *Report of the Committee on One-Parent Families*, Cmnd. 5629, London, HMSO (1974).
77. On 9 July 1981, the Government stated that 'about half of those families who were thought to be eligible for FIS were one-parent families' (*Hansard*, Written Answers, col. 1210).
78. Child Benefit Act 1975.
79. B.L. Harvey, *Income Tax 1982/83*, Croydon, Tolley Publishing Company (1983).
80. N.A.D. Lambert and J. Matthewman, *Social Security and State Benefits 1982/83*, Croydon, Tolley Publishing Company (1983).
81. Social Security Pensions Act 1975. This followed a White Paper, *Better Pensions* (Cmnd. 5713, London, HMSO, 1974).

82. See R. Hemming and J.A. Kay, 'The Costs of the State Earnings Related Pension Scheme', *Economic Journal* (June 1982).
83. For a discussion of the implications of contracting out see R. Hemming and J.A. Kay, 'Contracting Out of the State Earnings Related Pension Scheme', *Fiscal Studies*, 2/3 (November 1981).
84. 'National Superannuation: Labour's Policy for Security in Old Age', London, Labour Party (1957).
85. See Ogus, op. cit., for a discussion.
86. The White Paper was *National Superannuation and Social Insurance* (Cmnd. 3883, London, HMSO, 1969), the main provisions of which became the National Insurance and Superannuation Bill 1969.
87. For a discussion, see A. Maynard, in M.H. Cooper (ed.), *Social Policy: A Survey of Recent Developments*, Oxford, Blackwell (1974), especially pp. 188-9.
88. The White Paper was *Strategy for Pensions* (Cmnd. 4715, London, HMSO, 1971), which was to become the Social Security Act 1973.
89. Introduced by the Social Security Pensions Act 1975, based on the White Paper *Better Pensions*, op. cit.
90. Pensions in money terms were linked to the higher of earnings or prices, and so rose in real terms as real earnings rose.
91. The real value of the state retirement pension was slightly reduced in November 1983.
92. Earnings-related supplement to unemployment benefit was introduced on 6 October 1966.
93. Earnings-related supplement was finally abolished in January 1982.
94. Most recently in the 1983 Budget.
95. Unemployment benefit was brought into tax in July 1982.
96. National Insurance Surcharge was introduced in the Finance Act 1978.
97. *Report by the Government Actuary on the Draft Social Security Benefits Uprating Order 1981*, Cmnd. 8296, London, HMSO.
98. *Social Security Statistics 1981*, London, HMSO, Table 1.34.
99. *The Government's Expenditure Plans 1983/84 to 1985/86*, Cmnd. 8789-II, London, HMSO, Vol. 2, Table 2.12.3.
100. Beveridge, op. cit., paras. 217-32, pp. 84-90.
101. B.S. Rowntree, *Poverty and Progress: A Second Social Survey of York*, London, New York, and Toronto, Longman Green (1941).
102. G.D.H. Cole, *The Post-war Condition of Britain*, London, Routledge and Kegan Paul (1949), Chap. 15.
103. D. Seers, *Changes in the Cost of Living and the Distribution of Income since 1938*, Oxford, Blackwell (1949).
104. C.H. Feinstein, *Statistical Tables of National Income, Expenditure and Output 1855-1956*, Cambridge (1976), Table 62.
105. B.S. Rowntree and G.R. Lavers, *Poverty and the Welfare State*, London, New York, and Toronto, Longman Green (1951).

2
Problems with the Present System

British social security is like a patchwork quilt falling apart at the seams. It has evolved over two centuries in a haphazard manner; as problems have emerged, or compromises been necessary, new bits have been tacked on with inadequate thought about the overall structure. There are now simply too many benefits, administrative costs are extremely high, and many of those who need benefits are not receiving them despite the enormous resources devoted to their payment. As unemployment and the size of the pensioner population have risen, the strains on the system have multiplied. Today, social security has fallen into severe public disrepute.

What are the principal faults of the present system of social security and its interrelationship with taxation? The first and most fundamental failing is its inefficiency. It is inefficient in a number of senses. There is administrative inefficiency, in that there is a high degree of duplication between different branches of government engaged in similar, but poorly co-ordinated, activities. Information about household incomes is collected by the Inland Revenue, and by the Department of Health and Social Security (DHSS), and by local authorities. We have one income tax run by the Inland Revenue and another, national insurance contributions, run by the DHSS. We have a system of national insurance benefits, and a means-tested scheme of social assistance, and millions of households are entitled to both. There are many families who pay between 20 and 30 per cent of their income in direct taxes, and receive similar sums in benefits.

However, the high administrative cost of the system is only one — rather narrow — reflection of its inefficiency. More important is that it fails to achieve what it sets out to do. The problem of poor 'take-up' of means-tested benefits is well known, and we summarise available evidence on the extent of the problem in the following pages. The reverse problem[1] (popularly dubbed the 'black economy') occurs in the tax system when collection mechanisms fail, or when claimants benefit by inaccurately reporting their income or employment status. Even where benefits are correctly awarded according to the rules, it is not obvious that they achieve the original aims of the system. In many cases, means-tested benefits are received by those who would not be entitled to them on the basis of their current income. This is because benefits such as family income supplement (FIS) and housing benefit are assessed over a short period and paid for a much longer one. The result is a mismatch between benefit receipt and need. Many of those who need benefits do not receive them, and much of benefit expenditure is on those who do not need it. We examine this problem in detail later in this chapter.

These three aspects of inefficiency — high administrative cost, low take-up, and the payment of benefit to many who do not need it — are elements of a narrow, though important, view of efficiency; how successful is the system in terms of its own apparent objectives? How well does it succeed in giving, or collecting, what it sets out to give or collect? Chapter 4 will be concerned with improving efficiency in this sense, and with showing how an integrated tax and benefit system could deliver, cheaply and automatically, the income distribution which the present tax and social security systems set out to achieve.

It is still more important to ask whether the apparent objectives of the system are well chosen. Of course, the objectives of any social security system are many and complex. The one on which we concentrate is the prevention of poverty. Most people would, we believe, agree that a civilised society should attempt to secure some minimum standard of living for its citizens, regardless of their circumstances, or misfortunes, or indeed imprudence. There are other purposes for social security which are subsidiary, and perhaps more controversial. Should the state intervene to help people redistribute their income over their lifetime, or to help them to support their children? There are also ways in which the system may need to have regard to other objectives of economic policy, such as the incentive to work, or to save. But it is for its effects on poverty that the system should, we believe, principally be judged and, in this chapter, it is in these terms that we measure its efficiency.

Because development has been piecemeal, interaction between different benefits and between benefits and the tax system creates severe anomalies. It is these that give rise to the 'poverty' and 'unemployment' traps which are so popular in the Press. Although this set of problems has received considerable attention recently — not least in the inquiry of the Select Committee on the Treasury and Civil Service[2] — we rehearse the problems in this chapter and provide some evidence on their extent.

We also consider state pension provision in the future, and in particular the State Earnings-Related Pension Scheme (SERPS). At present, demographic trends are favourable to pension provision, and the scheme is young. Problems for financing of pensions do not emerge until after the year 2000, but then they will be very serious. On reasonable demographic and other assumptions, the burden on the working populations will then be very great. The price implied might be worth paying if the scheme would solve, or alleviate, many of the problems of UK social security today; as we show, it is essentially irrelevant to them.

Inefficiency in administration

We now have two direct tax systems — income tax, administered by the Inland Revenue, and national insurance contributions, administered by the DHSS — and various benefit systems: a national insurance benefit system paying pensions, unemployment, sickness, and other benefits; supplementary benefit (SB); and a plethora of specialised means-tested benefits — family income supplement for those in work, housing benefit (administered by local authorities), and a multitude of benefits in kind. So poor families in work pay two direct taxes on income and are likely to have their incomes made up by three distinct benefits as well as being entitled to three or more benefits in kind. Unemployed families receive benefit from four possible different sources, each administered separately.

It is not surprising that administrative costs are high. To administer the main means-tested benefit, supplementary benefit, costs over 10p per £1 of benefit paid, while national insurance benefits cost between 1½p and 8p. Duplication of effort leads to far more effort than seems necessary being expended to administer social security not very well. Table 2.1 summarises the evidence we have been able to find on just how much social security administration costs, and makes some comparison with what it cost ten years ago. The table compares the administrative cost of the system in 1981/2 with that of 1971/2. It shows that, in 1981/2 prices, administrative costs rose from £720 million to £1,145 million. However, this increase was more than balanced by increased benefit payments; the overall administrative cost as a percentage of total payments fell from 4.6 per cent in 1971/2 to 4.2 per cent in 1981/2. Broadly, administrative costs relative to payment in 1981/2 were much the same as they were ten years earlier; there has been some improvement in administration of the national insurance benefits, but this has been outweighed by an increasing number of people

TABLE 2.1

Administrative costs of the benefit system 1971-1981

	£m. at 1981/2 prices*		£ per £1 of benefit payment‡	
	1971/2†	1981/2	1971/2	1981/2
Supplementary benefit	249	507	0.104	0.105
Family income supplement	–	3	–	0.045
Unemployment benefit	85	142	0.096	0.083
Sickness benefit/ invalidity benefit	137	139	0.089	0.067
Retirement pension	97	180	0.013	0.015
Attendance allowance	–	14	–	0.042
Mobility allowance	–	5	–	0.029
Non-contributory invalidity pension	–	7	–	0.056
Others	152	148	0.049	0.025
Total, above benefits	720	1,145 §	0.046	0.042

Notes:

* These figures were supplied on request by the DHSS. No earlier figures than 1971/2 are available.

† Converted to 1981/2 prices by the Retail Price Index.

‡ Calculated from DHSS numbers and expenditure on benefit given in, for 1971/2, *Social Security Statistics 1973* (London, HMSO) and, for 1981/2, *The Government's Expenditure Plans 1983/84 to 1985/86,* Table 2.12 Cmnd. 8789, London, HMSO.

§ This figure matches, broadly, the figure for overall administrative costs given in *The Government's Expenditure Plans 1983/84 to 1985/86,* Table 2.12. They are broken down as NI fund administration (£699 m.), DHSS non-contributory benefits administration (£398 m.), and local authority administration (£46 m.).

dependent on – the more expensive to administer – supplementary benefit.

A small amount of evidence on administrative costs and manpower is available from sources other than those of Table 2.1, largely through Parliamentary questions. In 1978/9, the administrative cost of paying benefits to the unemployed was stated to be 10.5p in the pound for unemployment benefit and 18p for supplementary benefit,[3] rather above the figures shown in Table 2.1 for all recipients. Some 35,000 staff are employed in DHSS local offices administrating supplementary benefit.[4] A further 30,999 administer contributory benefits, with another 2,300 providing ancillary services.[5] Administrative costs per unit of payment have remained at similar levels since 1981/2; in 1983/4 administrative costs are forecast to be £1,379 million (or £1,220 million in 1981/2 prices).[6] In 1983/4, total benefit payment will be some £32,885 million, implying no change in cost per unit from 4.2 per cent. For purposes of comparison, the cost of income tax collection is approximately 2 per cent of revenue.

The evidence reported here is by no means an exhaustive examination of the administrative cost of the system. However, it reflects as much information as we have been able to glean from (published or unpublished) official sources. As Sir Derek Rayner said in his recent paper: 'A paucity of management information has been one barrier to the effective management of resources in central government departments.'[7]

Two clear facts emerge from Table 2.1. First, supplementary benefit, with administrative costs of £500 million, or 10 per cent of total payments, is very expensive to administer. Second, despite technological advances in both payment and calculation of entitlement, administrative costs per unit of payment have remained fairly constant over the last ten years. This is largely because any gains from increased efficiency have been swallowed by increasing dependence on — expensive — means-tested benefits.

Very broadly, the costs of running a benefit system are directly related to the frequency and complexity of deciding who is entitled to receive payments. This cost is in addition to the cost of the parallel exercise of collecting money from taxpayers. When a large number of benefit recipients receive benefits from more than one source, each with its own assessment procedures (and in 1983/4 21 per cent of the recipients of unemployment benefit and 15 per cent of retirement pensioners also received supplementary benefit[8]), and when, in addition, a large number of benefit recipients also pay tax, it is not surprising that administrative costs are very high. The proposals outlined later in this book would reduce significantly the number and complexity of individual assessments; the scope for drastic savings in administrative costs is large. Integration of the tax and benefit systems, as described in this book, replaces means tests, contribution conditions, tax assessments, and national insurance contributions by a single income assessment.

Although the argument for administrative simplification is self-evident from an examination of what happens at present, there is also some reason to believe that the situation will deteriorate further if the present system is left unchanged. The gradual erosion of tax thresholds relative to wages, moves towards full economic pricing of council houses and fuel, and the increasing probability of spells of unemployment and of unusual employment patterns will all tend to increase such overlaps as exist at present. Attempts to deal with the increasing strain that these changes have put on the system in a piecemeal manner have not been very successful so far; the ill-fated housing benefit scheme, introduced in 1983, has now become a byword for the ineptitude of the system.

An obvious method of improving the efficiency of the system is to introduce new technology. Attempts to introduce computers into UK tax administration date back to the early 1960s, when there were plans to build a network of regional computer centres. The first to be completed, in East Kilbride in Scotland, suffered extensive teething problems, while the second, at Bootle, experienced serious delays during implementation. Plans for further centres were then abandoned. The proposal of the tax credit scheme in the early 1970s meant that further computerisation was deferred until the details of this scheme had been worked out.

Work on a new set of plans for computerisation began in 1977, and the implementation of the new system is now under way. Full operation is likely around the end of the decade. The new plans involve the creation of twelve regional centres. Each local tax office will have some limited processing capability and be linked directly to one of the regional centres. Eventually these regional centres will be linked together.

Although it is clear that computerisation of the income tax system is long overdue, it is less clear that the particular form of computerisation that has been chosen is the most appropriate for the future. Much of the delay and expense in introducing computers is caused by the need to link local offices together. To a large extent this is because of the movements operation: in order to be able to run PAYE (Pay As You Earn) on a cumulative basis, employees who move from one job to another need to be monitored throughout the year. If on the other hand we had a system of individual provision of information and end-year assessment, such as that proposed in this book and operated in all countries except the UK and Eire, the movements operation would be strictly limited.

A strategy for the computerisation of the DHSS and Department of Employment administration of the benefit system was outlined in a report in 1982.[9] This describes the development of a computer network for the benefit system, incorporating existing computers which administer state pensions and national insurance records (mostly centralised at Newcastle upon Tyne). This network will also link local offices to one of several 'area computers' which will all be linked to a central claimant index held at Newcastle upon Tyne. The report discusses very briefly the possibility of some sort of tax credit scheme, but assumes that if this is implemented — which it regards as 'by no means certain, not least in view of the high potential cost' — the administration will occur by communication between Newcastle upon Tyne and the central Inland Revenue computer.

The computers now being installed by the Inland Revenue or planned by the DHSS do not seem the most appropriate for the administration of a scheme such as that described in this book. The administration of a system of benefit credits in conjunction with PAYE is essentially very simple: it could be achieved on microcomputers at a very local level or by one (or more) large computer. The complexity of the computer systems we are about to acquire is largely because they are designed to administer the present, very different, system. We find this a worrying development, and a potentially serious obstacle to sensible reform; it is very likely that, once the new computers are in place, 'high potential cost' will be used as a strong argument against any reform at all. We are using modern technology for purposes which the technology itself makes obsolete; but the management structure of Government departments appears to be one in which this issue does not emerge.

Inefficiency in operation

To receive their full entitlement to benefit, poor families may have to claim from numerous different sources. In some cases the reward for following complicated claims procedures may be quite small. Families may not have heard of a particular benefit or they may be so overawed by the system's complexity that they do not claim their entitlement. Some may feel that it is wrong to claim certain benefits, like supplementary benefit, which are described as non-contributory.

Whatever the reasons, the record on take-up is not good. Although it is a hazardous business to estimate how many people are entitled to benefit but do not receive it, Table 2.2 summarises what evidence there is. According to the most recent Government estimates, only 50 per cent of those entitled to FIS, 70 per cent of those entitled to rent and rate rebates, and 74 per cent of those entitled to supplementary benefit actually receive these benefits. A recent study of poverty[10] estimated that, despite a system which is intended to keep everyone's incomes above a particular level (the SB scale rate, after housing), in 1976 some 910,000 families had incomes below this level and 'needed' £220 million (£470 million in 1983 prices) to bring them to SB levels. The most recent government figures[11] suggest that in 1977 some 1.3 million families had incomes below the SB line.

TABLE 2.2
Estimates of take-up of various benefits
(recipients as percentage of those estimated entitled)[1]

	Most recent Government estimate		National Consumer council* 1974/5	†Townsend 1976
Supplementary benefit				
All recipients	74	(1977)‡	48 Local	60–65
Pensioners	65	(1979)§	75 National	
Rent rebates	72	(1979)¶	45–60 Local	Under 30
			70–75 National	
Rent allowances	50	(1979)¶	<40	
Rate rebates	70	(1979)¶	<40 Local	
			65 National	Under 25
Family income supplement	50	(1978/9)‖	<40 Local	
			75 National	
Free school meals			65–80	60
Free welfare foods	4	(1977)**		
Free welfare meals				Under 2
One-parent benefit	70	(1981)††		

Sources and notes:

*This study contrasts the results of local surveys and 'official' national estimates (National Consumer Council, *Means-Tested Benefits*, London, NCC, 1977).

†*Poverty in the United Kingdom,* Harmondsworth, Penguin (1979), Table 25.18, p. 892. Townsend disregards from the numerator all those who are receiving the 'wrong' amount.

‡*Hansard,* 28 October 1980, col. 268.

§*Hansard,* 2 February 1983, col. 128. Based on 1979 Family Expenditure Survey.

¶ *Hansard,* 1 December 1980, col. 88. Based on 1979 Family Expenditure Survey.

‖*Social Security Statistics 1981.*

**Hansard*, Written Answers, 28 October 1980, col. 269.

††*Social Security Statistics 1982.*

Both FIS and the housing benefits were introduced to supplement existing benefits and bring the incomes of poor families in work up to a minimum level. The low take-up of both these benefits indicates that they are not doing their job very well; however, they conceal a deeper problem. Not only do these benefits fail to reach many of those who are entitled to them, but also they are paid to others with higher incomes, despite the fact that they are ostensibly means tested.

The problem arises because both FIS and housing benefit are assessed on income over a short period but continue to be paid for a much

TABLE 2.3
Recorded benefit receipt compared with entitlement based on current income, 1981
Estimated numbers ('000)

	Receiving but not entitled	Receipt over 20% larger than entitlement	Receipt within 20% of entitlement	Receipt over 20% smaller than entitlement	Entitlement but no receipt	% total 'non take-up'	% receipt 'not needed'
Rent rebates	67 (2.87)	198 (6.10)	560 (6.66)	706 (4.74)	648 [3.45]	30.7	4.4
Rate rebates	195 (1.25)	585 (2.28)	1,677 (2.39)	1,160 (1.46)	2,625 [1.57]	43.4	5.4
Family income supplement	60 (5.69)	15 (9.87)	21 (11.75)	21 (7.98)	108 [8.47]	65.5	51.2

Source: IFS analysis of the 1981 Family Expenditure Survey.

Notes: (i) Average receipt in round brackets ( ), entitlement in square [ ].

(ii) The receipts recorded on the Family Expenditure Survey are the answer to the question 'Was there a rebate on your last rent/rate payment?' Entitlement is calculated using the benefit rates applying to date of interview, using information on household current incomes and characteristics. Multiple tax-unit households and those currently receiving supplementary benefit are excluded from the analysis. Pensioners and those currently unemployed are excluded from the FIS analysis.

(iii) 'Non take-up' is the ratio of those entitled but not receiving to all those who are estimated as entitled. 'Not needed' is the ratio of those receiving but not entitled to those receiving.

longer one. For FIS, the period of assessment is five weeks and of payment one year, while rent and rate rebates are in principle re-assessed every six months.[12] The result is that those whose income fluctuates considerably can claim benefit during periods of low income, but continue to receive benefit when their income is higher. In Table 2.3 we present the results of a comparison between recorded current receipt of FIS and rent and rate rebates in 1981 and estimated entitlement to these benefits based on the unit's recorded income. The third column shows that only 37 per cent of those receiving rent rebates, 46 per cent of those receiving rate rebates, and 18 per cent of those receiving FIS are receiving within 20 per cent of their estimated entitlement. The penultimate column gives our estimates of non take-up.

These estimates compare the number of households estimated as entitled to benefit on the basis of their current income but not receiving benefit with the total estimated as entitled. Some 31 per cent of those entitled to rent rebates, 43 per cent of those entitled to rate rebates, and a remarkable 66 per cent of those estimated as entitled to FIS do not have any recorded receipt of these benefits. These figures are not directly comparable to the figures on take-up in Table 2.2; there the convention is usually to express the number receiving benefit (whether or not they are entitled on the basis of their current income) as a percentage of the total who are either entitled to or receiving benefit. On this basis, the 'take-up' estimates implied by Table 2.3 are 70 per cent for rent rebates, 58 per cent for rate rebates, and 48 per cent for FIS.[13]

Although attention is usually focused on take-up of benefits,[14] the mismatch between receipt and entitlement indicated by this analysis is equally revealing. Because incomes fluctuate, or because benefit assessment procedures are inadequate, or because the information recorded on household surveys is not consistent with that recorded by benefit authorities, the majority of all recipients of the three benefits were, in the week interviewed, apparently receiving benefits of an amount which differed from their entitlement by at least 20 per cent. About 5 per cent of the recipients of rent and rate rebates and over 50 per cent of those receiving FIS appear to be receiving benefit at a time when their current income would not entitle them to it.

Although we are confident that the qualitative picture presented above is not misleading, some care is necessary in interpreting the actual numbers. The results for FIS are based on a very small sample of households. Out of a total sample of some 7,500 households in the 1981 Family Expenditure Survey, only 55 recorded receipt of FIS and a further 51 households would, we estimate, be entitled to benefit but do not receive it. In addition, although the income definitions we have used are carefully designed to match those actually used for assessing the available resources of the household, the Family Expenditure Survey is not primarily concerned with estimating benefits, so we might expect, for those with static incomes, the benefit authorities to do it rather better.

The evidence reported here indicates that the two means-tested benefits intended to keep the income of the working poor above a minimum level are inefficient on two counts. First, because of low take-up, many of those who are currently poor are not receiving the benefits and, second, because the benefits are assessed on income over a relatively short period but received over a much longer one, some of the expenditure on benefits is being 'wasted' in periods when people do not need it to bring their income to above the minimum level, while others are not receiving enough to cover their needs. The reforms suggested later in this book would significantly ease the first problem and eliminate the second.

Problems with the 'inefficiency' of the benefit system are not confined to FIS and rent and rate rebates. It is a central contention of this book that the role of the UK benefit system is now somewhat confused. Although we still pay lip-service to the idea that benefits received when unemployed, sick or old are somehow the result of our own contributions at other times, the relationship between contributions and eventual receipt is very weak, and in 1982/3[15] 63 per cent of the unemployed and 19 per cent of pensioners had their incomes determined not by national insurance benefits but by the means-tested supplementary benefit.[15] It is clear that the state's role has increasingly become one of guaranteeing a minimum income to all whose other incomes are too low. But the combination of benefits that currently exist for this purpose do so inadequately and at excessive cost.

Figure 2.1 shows the incomes of four different families, and compares them to a poverty level (which may, but need not, be the SB line). Family A does not take up any benefits, and remains 'poor' after all benefits. Family B receives some benefits — probably national insurance benefit and child benefit — but fails to claim, or is not entitled to, benefits sufficient to bring it to the poverty line, so that it too remains poor. Family C has enough other income for the benefits it receives — child benefit and national insurance again — to bring its net income above the poverty line. Finally, family D was not poor before benefits, but still receives them. If the benefit system was merely intended to make sure no one was poor, then only (V) and (W) would be needed, while (X) and (Y) are 'wasted'.

In Table 2.4 we evaluate some of the areas in Figure 2.1 We do this

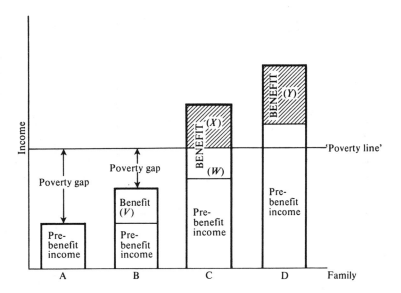

Fig. 2.1 Proportion of benefits 'needed' to bring incomes above poverty line

by identifying those whose recorded income before benefits in the 1981 Family Expenditure Survey is below their SB scale rate plus housing costs, and estimating what proportion of benefits paid is used to bring the incomes of poor families to that level. We call families like A and B – who remain poor even after the benefits which they receive – the 'post-benefit poor', while a household like C, whose poverty is eliminated by benefits, is described as the 'pre-benefit poor'.

The table shows how the benefits, other than supplementary benefit (which we have assumed performs its job perfectly for those who receive it), contribute to bringing incomes to above the relevant SB level. Only those received by the post-benefit poor and necessary to bring the incomes of the pre-benefit poor to the SB level are strictly required; all other benefits either increase incomes to above this level or are received by those who would not be poor anyway. Some 46 per cent of national insurance benefits other than the pension are shown by the analysis to be used in this way, while, for the reasons we have already discussed, only 32 per cent of FIS and rent and rate rebates perform this role. Neither the pension nor child benefit are actually intended as income assistance benefits, so judging them on this criterion may be somewhat harsh, but some 59 per cent of pensions and only 22 per cent of child benefit payments are actually necessary to keep their recipients out of 'poverty'.

TABLE 2.4

Proportion of benefits necessary to bring incomes to the supplementary benefit line in 1981

	Supplementary benefit*	National insurance (unemployment, sickness, etc.) benefits	FIS and rent and rate rebates	Pension	Child benefit	All benefits
Received by 'post-benefit poor'	–	7.7	20.3	14.9	6.2	11.1
Necessary to bring 'pre-benefit poor' to SB level	100.0	33.4	17.2	43.9	15.6	42.9
Extra received by 'pre-benefit poor'	–	13.4	20.4	15.0	2.4	11.7
Received by 'non-poor'	–	45.5	42.1	26.2	75.8	34.3
	100.0	100.0	100.0	100.0	100.0	100.0
Total payments (£m. 1981/2†)	4,835	4,828	620	12,126	3,448	25,857

*See Note (ii) below.

†*The Government's Expenditure Plans 1983/84 to 1985/86.*

The total 'income deficiency' of post-benefit poor in 1981 was £1,300m.

Notes: (i) This analysis is carried out on a family-unit basis. So secondary units in a household may be regarded as 'poor' even if the rest of the household has adequate resources.

(ii) Although a comparison of characteristics and income from The Family Expenditure Survey does sometimes indicate that individuals are receiving supplementary benefit at the 'wrong' level, we have decided that in these cases we should give the DHSS the benefit of the doubt and so assumed that in all cases 'needs and resources' are adequately assessed.

(iii) Benefits are assumed to contribute to income in the following order: pension, child benefit, national insurance benefits, FIS, rent and rate rebates, supplementary benefit.

The message of this analysis is dramatic. Even if we assume, as in the table, that all recipients of supplementary benefit receive the 'right' amount, only 54 per cent of the benefits we actually pay are strictly necessary to bring incomes to the SB level — even though a significant proportion of benefit goes to people who have no other income at all. Another 12 per cent increases the incomes of those who would be poor without benefits, while 34 per cent is paid to people who would not be poor on the basis of their current income even if there were no benefit system. 42 per cent of FIS and rent and rate rebates, 46 per cent of national insurance benefits, 26 per cent of pensions, and over 75 per cent of child benefit goes to individuals and families who already have incomes above the SB level.

If the major aim of the benefit system is to keep incomes above some minimum level, then it is rather ineffective in doing so. Not only does low take-up mean that some people 'slip through the net', but a high proportion of benefit expenditure provides income in excess of this minimum. If our principal objective is to boost low incomes to an acceptable level, this could be done much more cheaply, and/or we could afford to be considerably more generous to the poor, if payments to those who do not strictly 'need' the money were curtailed. This is not to say that the state may not decide that it wishes to support certain activities — for instance the rearing of children, through child benefit — irrespective of circumstances; however, when the price is so high, it should be clear precisely how it does, or does not, wish to spend money.

Anomalies and interactions

So far, we have been concerned with the effectiveness of benefits in achieving the goal of guaranteeing an income sufficient to meet needs. However, the interaction of many different benefits with distinct direct taxes can create serious anomalies. The most important of these problems are popularly dubbed the 'poverty trap' and the 'unemployment trap'.

The poverty trap hits households who can make themselves worse off by increasing their income. Benefits such as FIS and housing benefit are intended to increase the net income of households with insufficient resources for their needs. These benefits are gradually withdrawn as income rises. Table 2.5 shows how this withdrawal of benefit affects the net income of a couple with two children as gross income rises from £50 per week to £200 per week. If such a family were to claim all the benefits for which it is eligible, its net income would actually fall as its

TABLE 2.5

How a couple with two children* are affected by taxes and benefits
(1983/4, November 1983 benefits)

	Gross income (£ p.w.)				
	50	80	100	120	200
Plus:					
Child benefit	13.00	13.00	13.00	13.00	13.00
Housing benefit	22.55	17.60	13.89	8.29	–
Family income supplement	22.50	7.50	–	–	–
Free school meals	5.00	5.00	–	–	–
Less:					
Tax	–	–7.88	–13.88	–19.88	–43.88
National insurance	–4.50	–7.20	–9.00	–10.80	–18.00
Net income	108.55	108.C	104.01	110.61	151.12

*Rent £20 p.w., rates £7 p.w.

gross income rose from £50 per week to £100 per week. As income
rises by £1 in this range, income tax may be levied at 30p and national
insurance contributions at 9p. FIS entitlement may be reduced by 50p
and housing benefit by between 28p and 33p – cumulating to a possible
maximum of £1.05½.[16] In addition, eligibility for FIS 'passport' benefits,
such as free school meals, is lost when FIS is finally withdrawn.

This is clearly undesirable, but would matter little if there were no
households with sufficiently low gross incomes to be affected. It is
therefore important to examine, as we do in Figure 2.2, how many
households have incomes which place them in the poverty trap. Only
those eligible for FIS face such high marginal rates, and childless
households are unaffected by FIS. We can see from Figure 2.2 that very
few working families have incomes in this area. (In 1982/3, only
143,000 families received FIS.)

A related, but distinct, problem is the 'unemployment trap'. The
poverty trap applies to families whose net income would fall, or grow
only very slightly, if their gross income rose. The unemployment trap
affects low-income families who can find that they would be 'better off
on the dole' because their net income in work is lower than the value
of benefits they would receive if the breadwinner were unemployed.

The effect of the tax and benefit systems on the relationship between
incomes in and out of work is a subject which attracts hyperbole and
dubious analysis. Fears that incentives to seek or retain work are being

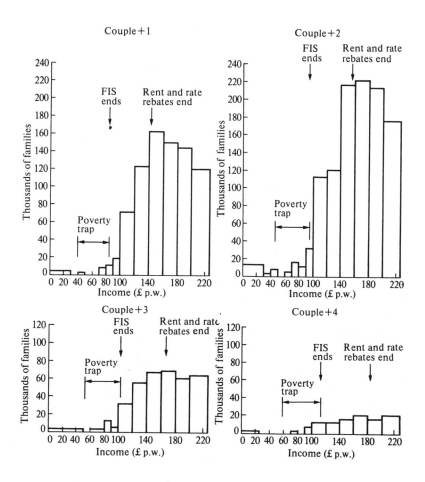

Fig. 2.2 Distribution of family incomes, 1983/4

blunted by an over-generous benefit system have contributed to decisions to abolish earnings-related supplements to unemployment benefit, to reduce the real value of unemployment benefit, and to make benefit receipt liable for income tax.

The importance of benefit incomes to work incentives, and the number of people who would be as well off if unemployed, is a subject of continuing controversy.[17] The debate centres on the calculation of 'replacement rates', which compare net incomes in and out of work for a given individual. A possible example calculation of this kind is given in Table 2.6: here our family with two children, earning £120 per week in work, would end up with 83 per cent of its net income if the

TABLE 2.6

The unemployment trap (November 1983)
Net income of a married man with two children*

In work	£ p.w.	Out of work	£ p.w.
Wage	120.00	Unemployment benefit	44.05
Child benefit	13.00	Child benefit	13.00
Housing benefit	8.29	Supplementary benefit	4.75
Tax	−19.88	Housing benefit	27.00
National insurance	−10.80	Expected tax rebate	3.00
Net income	110.61		91.80

Replacement rate = 91.80/110.61 = 83 per cent

*rent £20 p.w., rates £7 p.w.

head became unemployed. This 'replacement rate' for our particular family would be higher if income in work were lower, or if rent were higher, or if tax rebates were greater.

The only way to get a clear idea of how important replacement rates actually are is to attempt to measure them for a large and representative sample of the population. Choosing hypothetical households which generate a particular replacement rate proves very little about the overall extent of the problem. Unfortunately it is at the level of finding particular examples which generate high − or low − replacement rates that most of the policy debate is conducted.

Although some recent commentators have in the past stressed the impossibility of developing a single measure of an individual's replacement rate,[18] we would disagree with this view.[19] The effect on family incomes of a given-length spell of unemployment is a question which has, in principle, a well-defined and unambiguous answer. There is a stream of net income which he will enjoy if he remains in work, and a different stream of income and benefits which he will obtain if he does not. Actual estimation of the two streams may cause problems − not least for the individual concerned − but the principle of what such an estimation should be is clear.

In a recent article,[20] two of the present authors presented estimates of replacement rates and their development since 1968, based on a full sample of working family heads in the Family Expenditure Survey. The results, which relate to the 'average' effect of a short period (13 weeks) of unemployment and to the 'marginal' effect of the 53rd week of unemployment (an indication of the long-term position), are reproduced

TABLE 2.7

The development of replacement rates over time

	13-week average			53rd-week marginal		
	Average	% with > 0.9	% with < 0.5	Average	% with > 0.9	% with < 0.5
1968	0.870	35.2	0.5	0.537	2.8	30.7
1975	0.751	17.2	5.9	0.498	2.5	50.5
1978	0.790	21.0	2.3	0.519	2.2	44.0
1980	0.727	12.0	8.0	0.503	1.9	47.8
1982	0.597	3.2	28.0	0.510	2.2	52.3
1983	0.600	2.9	21.0	0.504	1.9	53.2

Source: A.W. Dilnot and C.N. Morris, 'Private Costs and Benefits of Unemployment': Measuirng Replacement Rates, in C.A. Greenhalgh, P.R.G. Layard, and A.J. Oswald (eds.), *The Causes of Unemployment*, Oxford, Oxford University Press (1984).

in Table 2.7. These estimates indicate that in 1983 very few people (2.9 per cent) would have received over 90 per cent of their income in work when they were unemployed for a short period, and even fewer in the long term. But this has not always been the case. As recently as 1978 some 21 per cent of working family heads had replacement rates in excess of 90 per cent. This was partly because of the tax rebates which tended to be received during short spells of unemployment. In 1978 unemployment benefit was not subject to income tax, so a period of unemployment meant that previous tax payments made while working would be refunded and liability on returning to work might be reduced. In 1978 there were also earnings-related supplements to benefit which boosted benefit receipt for the first six months of an unemployment spell. Earnings-related supplements were abolished in January 1982 and unemployment benefit was made taxable in July 1982. These two changes have caused a dramatic fall in average short-term replacement rates and in the number with replacement rates over 90 per cent.

The incentive problem which existed during the 1970s — that short periods of unemployment often carried little financial penalty — has largely been removed by recent policy changes. There has never been a serious problem over longer spells: throughout the period, long-term replacement rates have been, on average, as low as 50 per cent, and the proportion with long-term marginal rates in excess of 90 per cent has never been above 3 per cent.

The State Earnings-Related Pension Scheme

In Chapter 1, we described the political developments which had led to the introduction in 1978 of the State Earnings-Related Pension Scheme (SERPS).[21] If fully operational today, this scheme would add around one-third to the total social security budget. If finance of this magnitude were available, it is likely that the Beveridge proposals could be implemented on a scale which would substantially correspond to the hopes initially entertained for the scheme, and that many of the problems described in this chapter would thereby be removed. Alternatively, it could finance tax cuts of an order of magnitude which would considerably alleviate the interaction between the tax and social security systems. We could envisage, for example, a 60 per cent increase in national insurance benefits, a reduction in the basic rate of income tax to 20 per cent, or a 75 per cent increase in tax thresholds.

Unfortunately a detailed analysis of the effects of SERPS on income distribution and on incentives, of the kind which we undertake for other measures described in this book, is impossible. The reason is that because SERPS benefits depend on earnings profiles over a working lifetime, an assessment of their impact requires information about these profiles. Some such data could in principle be derived from the national insurance records maintained by the DHSS, but this source is not available, and has not been used for these purposes by the Department or by others; in particular, work of this type was not undertaken at the time when SERPS was introduced. We can therefore only describe the likely impact of the scheme in hypothetical terms.

Table 2.8 shows how an 'average' couple might be affected by SERPS. All figures are quoted at current prices, to avoid issues raised by the complex provisions for indexation. The husband earns £180 per week, around average male earnings; his wife completes 20 years of earnings and on average obtains about £100 per week during that time. If he were due to retire now, the husband might expect an occupational pension of £30 per week; in future, occupational pensions will be a good deal higher and we have put his entitlement at £50 per week, of which £25 is the guaranteed minimum pension (GMP) from his contracted-out scheme.

Such a couple will gain considerably from SERPS. Not only will the husband obtain a partial state earnings-related pension in addition to his occupational pension, but his wife would also be entitled to a pension and earnings-related pension in her own right. The gross income of the couple in retirement would rise from £85 to £152 per week. Table 2.9 shows the effect on their net income, assuming a typical

TABLE 2.8

Effect of the State Earnings-Related Pension Scheme on an average couple *

HUSBAND:	Earns £180 per week during working life
	Gets £30 per week occupational pension *now*
	Gets £50 per week occupational pension *then*
	of which £25 is GMP
WIFE:	Earns £100 per week for 20 years
	No occupational pension

NOW		*AFTER SERPS*	
Couple's state pension	£55	Husband's state pension	£51
Occupational pension	£30	Husband's occupational pension	£50
		Wife's state pension	£51
	£85		£152

*Illustrative figures based on November 1983 benefit levels.

5 per cent employee pension contribution. It falls from £194 while working to £138 in retirement and, bearing in mind that family responsibilities will have disappeared by this stage of the average couple's lifetime, their retirement standard of living will clearly be high in relation to that which they enjoyed in work. The husband's occupational pension, which is less than 30 per cent of final salary, is not a particularly good one.

By contrast, Table 2.10 shows the position of a poor couple, where the husband earns £120 per week and his wife's income is relatively small. This couple obtains just enough earnings-related pension to wipe out their current entitlement to supplementary pension. Assuming they were obtaining this pension, they will be little, if any, better off; the

TABLE 2.9

Effect on net income of an average couple *

Working	£ p.w.	Retirement	£ p.w.
Income	280	Income	152
Tax	−55	Tax	−14
National insurance	−22		
Pension contribution	−9		
Net income	£194	*Net income*	£138

*Illustrative figures based on 1983/4 tax system and November 1983 benefit levels.

TABLE 2.10
*Effect of the State Earnings-Related Pension Scheme on a poor couple**

HUSBAND:　Earns £120 per week during working life
　　　　　　No occupational pension

WIFE:　　　Only small part-time earnings after marriage

(Rent and rates £20 per week)

NOW		AFTER SERPS	
State pension	£55	State pension	£77
Supplementary pension	£20		
	£75		£77

*Illustrative figures based on November 1983 benefit levels.

principal contribution that SERPS makes to the position of the poorest pensioners is that for many it will solve the problem of poor take-up of existing entitlement to supplementary pension.

The cost of SERPS builds up only slowly. Table 2.11 presents estimates, prepared in 1982 at IFS and based on middle-of-the-road demographic assumptions, of how these costs may develop. The top line, which gives the 'support ratio', or number of working people per pensioner, shows that the demographic problems begin at the end of this century. By 2033, the support ratio will have fallen from 3.03 in 2001 to 2.4. This trend is reflected in the next line, which shows the tax rate required on the present contribution base to pay pensions, assuming the level of the pension stays in line with earnings. The third line shows how much of the final liability of the scheme will have been reached in each year; this rises from 20 per cent in 1991 to 90 per cent in 2033. This is reflected in the fourth line, which shows that the tax rate required to pay for the earnings-related part of state pensions will rise from 2 per cent in 1991 to over 10 per cent by 2033. Overall, the tax rate required to pay for pensions will rise from some 16 per cent in 1991 to over 27 per cent in 2033.

We imagine any dispassionate reader will share our bewilderment at the introduction of SERPS. We doubt if the resources required to implement it are available, and if they are, we should not wish to spend them on this form of indiscriminate largesse to the elderly. Deployed in other ways, they could transform the social security system, or the tax system, or the interaction between them. Deployed in this way, they do not even solve the principal weakness in current pension pro-

TABLE 2.11

The changing costs of state pensions

(Expressed as proportion of contribution base)

	1991	2001	2011	2023	2033	Steady-state
Support ratio	2.87	3.03	2.99	2.66	2.40	2.69
Cost of basic pension	13.9	13.2	13.4	15.0	16.7	14.9
Percentage of final SERPS: liability reached	*20*	*45*	*65*	*80*	*90*	*100*
Cost of SERPS	2.0	4.2	6.2	8.5	10.6	10.6
Cost of state pensions	15.9	17.4	19.6	23.5	27.3	25.5

Source: Based on figures in R. Hemming and J.A. Kay, 'The Costs of the State
Earnings Related Pension Scheme', *Economic Journal*, **92** 366 (1982).

vision. Even when SERPS is mature, there will still be — barring other changes — many pensioners below the SB level, workers penalised for changing jobs, and elderly people who see their standard of living in retirement eroded year by year through inflation. It is difficult to discuss the future of social security rationally in the shadow of this foolish commitment.

Appendix: A short description of the tax and benefit systems

I: *Direct taxes on income*

Income tax. Broadly, income tax is levied on all income arising in the United Kingdom and on the income of UK residents which arises abroad. The tax is assessed on an annual basis, with the year running from 6 April to the following 5 April. Almost all income is taxable — exceptions are interest on National Savings Certificates, Save As You Earn, some benefits (for example family income supplement, but not unemployment benefit, or supplementary benefit paid to the un-employed for the head of a family and his spouse), and luncheon vouchers (up to 75p a week). From taxable income, certain allowances are deducted. These are a fixed amount depending on family status. In 1983/4 the main allowances were:

Single	£1,785 p.a.
Couple	£2,795 p.a.
Additional personal	£1,010 p.a.
Single, age	£2,360 p.a.
Couple, age	£3,755 p.a.

The additional personal allowance is available to one-parent families, the age allowances to anyone over 65 (in the case of a couple, where either is over 65). There are a number of other allowances (for example the housekeeper's allowance) which are smaller, and of diminishing importance.

In addition to the allowances, certain expenses are allowed as deductions from taxable income. The most significant is interest payments on mortgages, but life assurance premia and occupational pension contributions are also allowable.

Income tax is then levied on taxable income after deductions of allowances and allowable expenses. It is calculated by applying a rate schedule as follows:

Rate of tax	Slice of taxable income (£)
30	14,600
40	−17,200
45	−21,800
50	−28,900
55	−36,000
60	36,000+

In addition to the rates of tax shown here, a surcharge of 15 per cent is payable on unearned income in excess of £7,100.

Since 1803, income has been split for purposes of tax assessment into six schedules:

A   Income from property.
B   Income from commercial woodlands.
C   Certain interest and annuities paid out of public revenue.
D   Income from trades, businesses and professions.
E   Wages and salaries.
F   Dividends and other distributions made by companies.

The vast majority of the country's working population pays tax under Schedule E. It is for this schedule that Pay As You Earn (PAYE) operates. PAYE is a method of cumulative withholding of tax from income. It is cumulative in the sense that it keeps a running tally of income received, tax paid, and allowances used, and operates so as to withhold the correct amount of tax at each payment. If under- or over-payment occurs one week, this is corrected in the next wage packet. As such it is very convenient for taxpayers, but unwieldy and costly to administer.

The schedular system of assessment introduces many anomalies, but the most significant is the timing complication introduced by Schedule D. The precise effects are extremely complex, but perhaps the best approximation to a description is that tax is paid on a preceding-year basis, at least one year (and often longer) after Schedule E payments. This is a gross simplification, but is obviously a cause of inequity, especially in periods of high inflation; the net result is an interest-free loan from the Exchequer to Schedule D taxpayers.

National insurance contributions. It is often claimed that national insurance (NI) contributions are not a tax. In principle, they are paid so that the individual becomes entitled to benefit from the national insurance scheme. However, since they are a compulsory payment out of income to the Government, and as the link between contributions and receipt is extremely weak, it seems difficult to defend such a statement.

The level of a person's contributions, and the relevant payment rules, depend on the class of contributions paid. There are four classes:

Class 1 Percentage-based contributions payable by most employees who earn more than the national insurance floor of £32.50 per week in 1983/4.

Class 2 Flat-rate contributions paid by self-employed people with profits of more than £1,690 p.a.

Class 3 Flat-rate voluntary contributions which can be paid to boost an otherwise insufficient contribution record.

Class 4 Percentage-based contributions payable by self-employed people, in addition to Class 2 contributions on profits between £3,800 p.a. and £12,000 p.a.

Broadly, if an individual is employed, is over 16 but under pension age, and earns more than the 'lower earnings limit' (LEL) both he and his employer are liable to Class 1 contributions. The level of contribution is calculated as a percentage of the employee's earnings up to the 'upper earnings limit' (UEL), provided they exceed the lower earnings limit.

Once earnings exceed the upper earnings limit (currently £235 p.a.) no additional liability is incurred. It is possible for an employee's job to be 'contracted out' of SERPS by an employer, who must then provide an occupational pension scheme. Such contracting out confers a lower rate of state national insurance contributions. In 1983/4 the rates were as follows:

Lower earnings limit	£ 32.50
Upper earnings limit	£235.00

	Normal	Contracted out
Employee contributions	9%	6.85%
Employer contributions	10.45%	6.35%

In addition, a surcharge of 1 per cent was payable by employers.

All self-employed people over 16 must, unless covered by some exemption, pay Class 2 and 4 contributions. As noted, Class 2 contributions are paid as a flat rate, Class 4 as a percentage of a band of profits.

II. Benefits available to those in work

Child benefit. Child Benefit is a non-contributory, flat-rate, weekly benefit payable for each qualifying child. Broadly, entitlement depends on residence in Great Britain; the claimant must have the child claimed for living with him or her, or be contributing to the child's maintenance. Child benefit is payable to children under 16, or under 19 if still at school. Child benefit will normally be paid to the mother. In addition to child benefit, one-parent benefit is paid to single parents receiving child benefit. From November 1983 the rates were:

Child benefit	£6.50 p.w.
One-parent benefit	£4.05 p.w.

Family income supplement. FIS is a non-contributory cash benefit payable to low-income families with children, provided the head of the family is in full-time paid work (defined as 30 hours per week, or 24 if the individual concerned is a single parent). Entitlement depends on the family's income falling below a certain limit. Benefit is assessed, normally over a period of five weeks, and then paid for a year before review. The amount payable is half the difference between the family's income and the relevant limit. The limits from November 1983 were:

Limit for a one-child family	£85.50 p.w.
Addition for each subsequent child	£ 9.50 p.w.
Maximum payment for a one-child family	£22.00 p.w.
Addition for each subsequent child	£ 2.00 p.w.

In addition to receipt of FIS, entitlement to FIS automatically confers the following 'passport' benefits:

Free milk and vitamins for pregnant and nursing women and young children.
Free school meals.
Free prescriptions.
Refund of hospital fares.
Free NHS spectacles.
Free NHS dental treatment.

Housing benefit. Housing benefit has recently replaced the system of rent and rate rebates which had been in operation in roughly the same form since 1972. For those in work, housing benefit makes a contribution to rent and rate payments, subject to a means test which compares a claimant's weekly income with a level of 'needs' determined by the size of his family. Entitlement to housing benefit is then calculated as 60 per cent of rent or rates plus (minus) a fraction of the excess (deficiency) of needs over income.

III. Benefits for those not in work

FIS is not available to families of which there is no working member, child benefit is paid automatically, and housing benefit is available subject to the rules outlined above.

Unemployment benefit. Unemployment benefit is a weekly flat-rate benefit, with additions for dependants (wife or children). Entitlement to unemployment benefit is by contribution record, and receipt lasts a maximum of 52 weeks. A claimant must be unemployed and fit for work, must register for work, and must not place 'unreasonable' restrictions on the kind of work he will accept. Unemployment benefit is not payable for the first three days of a spell of unemployment, and a claimant may be disqualified from benefit for up to six weeks in certain cases, such as loss of job through misconduct. Unemployment benefit has been taxable since July 1982.

Supplementary benefit. Supplementary benefit (SB) is intended as a 'safety net' to prevent anyone receiving an income below that which is felt to be a necessary minimum. It is a cash benefit which pays a claimant the difference between his net income and the relevant SB scale rate (the assessed level of need). The scale rate is determined by number of dependants, and certain additional requirements, with a higher level (the 'long-term' rate) applied to pensioners. Claimants must be 16 or over, and must not be in full-time work. They must not have savings or capital of over £3,000. Fit people below pensionable age are required to register for work, unless they have to remain at home to look after a child or relative. Receipt of supplementary benefit carries with it entitlement to the 'passport' benefits listed in the section on FIS.

Retirement pension – basic. The basic state retirement pension is paid at a flat weekly rate, with increases for dependants. Entitlement depends on the claimant's contribution record; a married woman or widow(er) can claim on the record of the spouse. Claimants must be over pensionable age (60 for women, 65 for men) and retired, or be at least five years over pensionable age. The amount of pension paid is reduced as the claimant's weekly earnings rise above £65 per week.

Additional retirement pension. Entitlement to the additional pension depends on the claimant having paid Class 1 contributions on earnings over the weekly lower limit in at least one tax year after 5 April 1978. The amount of earnings-related pension is based on a fraction of the revalued earnings from the 'best' twenty years of post-1978 earnings, and so the maximum will be received by no one until 1998.

Sickness benefit. Sickness benefit used to be payable to any person too ill to work provided the stoppage had lost them more than four days. Since the introduction of a new sickness benefit scheme in April 1983, employers are liable to pay sick pay, at at least a minimum level, for the first eight weeks of sickness in any tax year. When this period is over, liability to pay benefit becomes the state's responsibility.

Other benefits

There are many other benefits: invalidity benefit, industrial injury benefit, widows benefit, widows pension, maternity allowance, maternity grant, death grant, mobility allowance, attendance allowance, war pensions, and the various benefits in kind. Full details of these can be found in Lambert and Matthewman's *Social Security and State Benefits.*[22]

References and notes

1. For a discussion of this problem see A.W. Dilnot and C.N. Morris, 'What Do We Know About the Black Economy?', *Fiscal Studies*, 2/1 (March 1981). The latest official estimate was given by Sir William Pile in evidence to the House of Commons Expenditure Committee; he told it that it 'was not implausible that the black economy amounted to 7.5 per cent of GDP in 1977'. For further discussion see M. O'Higgins, 'Measuring the Hidden Economy: A Review of Evidence and Methodologies', Outer Circle Policy Unit, London (1980) and K. Macafee, 'A Glimpse of the Hidden Economy in the National Accounts' *Economic Trends* (February 1980). The most thoroughly researched US estimates are given in *Estimates of Income Unreported on Individual Tax Returns*, Washington DC, Internal Revenue Service (1979).

2. *The Structure of Personal Income Taxation and Income Support* (Report of the Subcommittee to the Treasury and Civil Service Select Committee), London, HMSO (May 1983), and see also C.N. Morris, The Structure of Personal Income Taxation and Income Support', *Fiscal Studies*, 3/3 (November 1982) and J.A. Kay and C.N. Morris, 'The IFS Position on Unemployment Benefits: A Reply', *Fiscal Studies*, 4/1 (March 1983).

3. 1978/9 estimates given in *Hansard*, Written Answers, 14 April 1980, col. 534.

4. 1983 estimate, given in *Hansard*, Written Answers, 1 May 1980, col. 650.

5. 1977 estimate, given in Supplementary Benefits Commission, *Annual Report 1979*, London, HMSO.

6. *The Government's Expenditure Plans 1983/84 to 1985/6*, London, HMSO, Vol. 2, Cmnd. 8789-II, Table 2.12.

7. *Efficiency and Effectiveness in the Civil Service* (Third Report of the Treasury and Civil Service Select Committee of the House of Commons), *Vol. 2, Evidence*, H.C. 236-II (1981/2).

8. *The Government's Expenditure Plans*, op. cit., Table 2.12.4.

9. *Social Security Operational Strategy: A Framework for the Future*, London, HMSO (1982).

10. W. Beckerman and S. Clark, *Poverty and Social Security in Britain since 1961*, London, Institute for Fiscal Studies (1982).

11. *Social Security Statistics 1982*, London, HMSO.

12. The rules for the various benefits are described in a number of publications, of which the most useful are *Welfare Rights Handbook*, London, Child Poverty Action Group (1983) and N.A.D. Lambert and J. Matthewman, *Social Security and State Benefits* 1982/3, Croydon, Tolley Publishing Company (1983).

13. The government's 50 per cent FIS figure appears to follow Townsend's *Poverty in the United Kingdom*, Harmondsworth, Penguin, 1979 methodology of excluding those who are no longer entitled but receiving.

14. See, for example, R. Simpson, 'Welfare Benefits', in F. Williams (ed.), *Why the Poor Pay More*, London, National Consumer Council (1977).

15. *The Government's Expenditure Plans*, op. cit., Table 2.12.4.

16. This is lower than a mere addition of the numbers would imply, for FIS is taken into account for housing benefit purposes.

17. Recent attempts to model the determinants of unemployment duration include A.B. Atkinson *et al.*, 'Unemployment, Social Security and Incentives', *Journal of Public Economics* (forthcoming); K. Burdett, 'Search, Leisure and Individual Labour Supply', in S. Lippman and J.J. McCall (eds.), *Studies in the Economics of Search*, Amsterdam, North Holland (1979); S.J. Nickell, 'The Effect of Unemployment and Related Benefits on the Duration of Unemployment', *Economic Journal*, 8 (March 1979); T. Lancaster, 'Econometric Model for the Druation of Unemployment',

Econometrica, **47** (1979); and M. Feldstein and J. Poterba, 'Unemployment Insurance and Reservation Wages', *Journal of Public Economics* (forthcoming). For a recent discussion of the importance of incomes out of work see D. Davies, A.P.L. Minford, and A. Sprague, 'The IFS Position on Unemployment Benefits', *Fiscal Studies* **3**/3 (November 1982) and Kay and Morris, op. cit.,

18. See, for example, A.B. Atkinson and N. Rau, 'The Specification of Income Taxation and Benefits in Models of Unemployment Duration', London School of Economics Unemployment Project Note No. 9, London, (LSE 1981) and Davies *et al.*, op. cit.

19. For a detailed discussion, see A.W. Dilnot and C.N. Morris, 'The Private Costs and Benefits of Unemployment', *Oxford Economic Papers* (November 1983).

20. Ibid.

21. The legislation was introduced in the Social Security Pensions Act 1975, but the scheme began operation in 1978.

22. Lambert and Matthewman, op. cit.

3

The Approach to Reform

A major part of this book is devoted to the development of a system which closely reproduces the existing net income distribution using a single-payment mechanism. Although this would, in our view, make the administration of social security considerably less expensive and more effective, for many critics of the present system it will seem to represent an undue preoccupation with the bathwater at the expense of the baby.

For them, the principal present fault is not that we do the right thing badly, but that we do the wrong thing. We have sympathy with this view, but we think it is important to try to distinguish the two issues. There are two reasons for this. One is that there is more prospect of achieving agreement on the structure of a social security system than on its objectives. The other is that the choice of objectives has in practice been constrained by the inefficiency of the structure. Each of these arguments deserves development.

Any serious proposal for social security reform needs quantitative illustration and costing, and such illustration will generally imply that some households gain and others lose from the changes. This makes it very difficult to separate the issue of how income distribution should be influenced from the issue of what income distribution should be the objective. Almost all proposals for introducing more rational mechanisms of income support have foundered on their failure to do this: changes which are both redistributive and administrative are inevitably resisted by those who would lose from the resulting redistribution. The root and branch reform of the system which has come closest to implementation is the 1972 tax credit scheme. It is instructive to note that the most sustained and influential critique of those proposals was entitled *The Tax Credit Scheme and the Redistribution of Income,*[1] and that tax credit schemes have subsequently been tagged as right-wing proposals. Yet it is easy to devise tax credit schemes which are more, less, or equally redistributive when compared to the status quo; there is no necessary connection between this particular mechanism and any particular income distribution.

It is for this reason that we devote a major part of this book to setting out the procedures which would achieve the objectives of the present tax and social security systems more effectively and more efficiently. In what follows, we spell out the structure of our proposed alternative and examine the extent to which the net income distribution it generates differs from that intended by the existing system. We show that under our proposed alternative, 88 per cent of working households would have net incomes within 1 per cent of their current levels. But an important by-product of a simpler and more transparent mechanism is that it is much easier both to consider sensibly whether this income distribution is the right one and to achieve alternatives.

Fundamental constraints

In the design of any tax or benefit system, there is an underlying conflict between equity and efficiency. This point is often greatly exaggerated. We operate things so badly at the moment that there is rarely any difficulty in pointing to reforms which would lead to gains in both. What is inefficient is usually also unfair, and vice versa. But there are several areas in which this conflict is inescapable, and we should begin by spelling out what they are and inviting the reader to reflect his own value judgements in his own choices.

In Chapter 2 we described the 'poverty trap' — the phenomenon by which households gain little or nothing from increasing their income. It is illustrated, schematically, in Figure 3.1. There are two, and only two, ways of grading a plateau like that shown in this figure. You lower one end, or raise the other. The former is shown by DB, and it makes the poorest households, such as those at D, substantially worse off. The alternative is shown by AE, and the problem here is that it raises the marginal rate of tax on those with incomes B and E. Unfortunately, although there are relatively few households in the poverty trap, as we move further up the income distribution towards E that distribution becomes increasingly dense. This means that we extend a milder version of the poverty trap to a much larger group of people (although many of these are actually made better off by the change).

We believe that marginal rates of tax in excess of 100 per cent are not only inefficient, but absurd and immoral. It is intolerable that poor people, endeavouring to improve their economic position by their own efforts, should find themselves worse off by a combination of complex events of which they may not understand the outcome, far less the mechanics. Nor can we share the view that the fact that they do not understand it makes it acceptable. In order to avoid

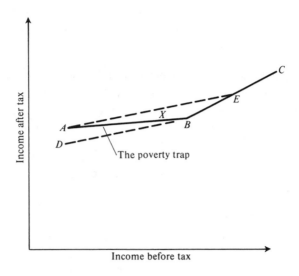

Fig. 3.1 The poverty trap

marginal rates in excess of 100 per cent, we believe we have to accept one or other of the disadvantages we describe. But we should hesitate before going much beyond that. It is certainly undesirable that there should be very high marginal rates of tax on the incomes of even a small group of poor people. But if the alternatives are either to make the poorest of these people considerably worse off, or to impose much greater disincentives to work on a much larger group, the cure may be worse than the disease. There is here an insoluble dilemma – we cannot guarantee a minimum standard of living without discouraging the work effort of those who, by their own devices, cannot obtain incomes much beyond that minimum.

Given the problems we have described in Chapter 2, it is hardly surprising that many radical proposals for root and branch reform of the social security system have been put forward. These fall under two main headings: 'back to Beveridge', and 'negative income tax'. These headings reflect the two principal ways in which a tax and benefit system can seek to relieve poverty. It can seek to identify the causes of poverty, or it can seek to identify the poor. The first of these approaches leads to the provision of *contingent* benefits – benefits to which you are entitled if some particular event occurs, like sickness, unemployment, or old age. The second of these approaches leads to *income-related* benefits, which you receive if you are poor, regardless of the reason for being poor. The advantage of the contingent benefit approach is that it avoids many of the problems of incentives and administration associated with means testing. The advantage of income-related benefits is that they are directly aimed at attacking poverty.

Many benefits are both contingent and income related. Family income supplement (FIS), for example, is payable only to those in work and supporting children. The amount received is then determined by income.

It is obvious that the extensive use of benefits which are both contingent and income related is likely to be a source of administrative complexity. The 'back to Beveridge' type of proposal attempts to resolve this by emphasising reliance on contingent benefits and reducing dependence on income-related, often disparagingly called 'means-tested', benefits. This is very much in line with the Beveridge proposal for social insurance with a fall-back scheme of national assistance. A negative income tax involves a move in just the opposite direction. It would scrap contingent benefits and make payments on the basis of the single criterion of whether or not your income indicates that you are poor.

By reducing the amount of information needed to operate a benefit system, both types of proposal hold promise of being simpler, more effective, and cheaper to run. But they do so at a high price. This is because they ignore information which enables us to target benefits much more effectively. The 'back to Beveridge' scheme would pay the same amount of pension or child benefit to all households, regardless of their income level. Either these amounts are very low, or the cost is very high. It was principally for this reason that, as we saw in Chapter 1, the original Beveridge scheme had failed to meet its objectives, and for this reason we do not think a 'back to Beveridge' move will occur, or is desirable.

Although the problems are less obvious, there are similar difficulties to be faced in any attempt to implement a negative income tax. A negative income tax is similar in effect to schemes which are called 'social dividend'[2] or 'basic income guarantee', and to some kinds of tax credit proposal. Figure 3.2 illustrates this equivalence. If there were no tax or benefit system, then income after tax would simply equal income before tax, and the 'tax schedule' would be shown by the line OA. Suppose tax is payable on income above the tax threshold OX. Then those with pre-tax incomes above OX will face a schedule BC. The higher the tax rate, the flatter will be the slope of BC. A negative income tax makes a payment of negative tax to those below OX. The tax schedule of BC is projected back through B, so that someone with no pre-tax income would now receive a payment of OD. In some

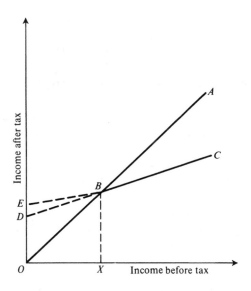

Fig. 3.2 Social dividend and negative income tax

versions of the proposal, the negative tax rate is higher than the positive rate. The government makes up a higher proportion of the shortfall from *OX* than it takes of the excess over *OX*. Such a schedule is illustrated by *EBC*.

Precisely the same effect could be achieved by giving everyone a social dividend of *OD*. This would be an unconditional payment to everyone, perhaps paid through the Post Office, and it would be financed by a tax schedule illustrated by the slope of *DBC*. If the social dividend were increased to *OE*, then this could be paid for by a higher rate of tax on the first *OX* of other income (thus reproducing the negative income tax schedule *EBC*) or, alternatively, by a higher general rate of tax.

In their simplest forms, social dividend or negative income tax schemes could dispense altogether with contingent information. Tax payment, or benefit receipt, would depend only on income, and not at all on characteristics such as old age, unemployment, or idleness. In Figure 3.3(a) we illustrate how such a scheme could operate. The crosses represent the incomes of a relatively well-off group – call them the working households – while the circles describe a poorer group, say pensioners. Not all pensioners are poor, however, nor are all working households well off. The negative income tax treats pensioners and

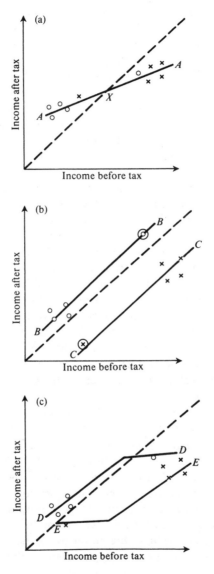

Fig. 3.3 Alternative tax systems

workers in just the same way, and everyone is on the negative income tax schedule AA. The flat slope of AA indicates that the negative income tax rate is rather high and the disincentive to work correspondingly large. All those with incomes below X receive money, all those with incomes above pay.

Figure 3.3(b) shows how this disincentive can be greatly reduced if we have two separate schedules, one for pensions (*BB*) and one for workers (*CC*). Whatever their income, pensioners receive the same amount in benefit and workers pay the same amount in tax. The pensioner schedule is more generous, so that if a pensioner and a worker have the same income before tax, the pensioner will nevertheless have a higher income after tax. The slopes of *BB* and *CC* are much greater than that of *AA*. For both groups, an increase in pre-tax income will now have a larger effect than before on the post-tax income, so that marginal rates of tax are lower and incentives to work are correspondingly improved.

The effect on overall income distribution is much the same. The principal difference is for the two 'outliers', ringed in Figure 3.3(b). The well-off pensioner now does better than any other household, while the poor worker does worst of all. This is a difficulty with any social security scheme which uses only contingent information. It is harsh on poor members of relatively affluent groups, and over-generous to affluent members of poor groups. In just this way, the Beveridge scheme did not do enough for poor working households.

Figure 3.3(c) shows a possible means of overcoming this difficulty. By introducing kinks into the two schedules, we can reduce these anomalies in the income distribution without affecting marginal rates for the majority of the population. The price we pay is that of imposing high marginal rates of tax on 'outliers' — untypical members of particular groups.

Necessarily, these outliers are not very numerous, and these high marginal rates may be the price we have to pay for avoiding high marginal rates of tax on the population at large. It is instructive to note that, by accident or design, we have reached in the present system precisely the pattern of tax schedules shown in Figure 3.3(c). As a whole, the system is much more generous to pensioners than to working households, but it seeks to claw that generosity back through high marginal tax rates on rich pensioners (from the application of age allowance and the earnings rule to the state pension) and to give additional support, at the cost of high marginal rates, to poor working families.

The lesson is that a cost-effective social security system must use both contingent and income-related information. In their pure forms, both the 'back to Beveridge' and the negative income tax schemes involve either unacceptably low benefit levels, or impossibly high cost, reflected in high marginal rates of tax. Each benefits from being modified in the direction implied by the other. An inevitable consequence is that we cannot have a system as administratively simple as we would like; but that does not imply that we cannot order these matters considerably better than we do now.

Alternative routes to reform

The attempt to bring the tax and social security systems closer together is hardly new. Several schemes with this intention were submitted in evidence to the Treasury and Civil Service Committee,[3] and the appendices to its report are a convenient compendium of these ideas. The best general discussion of the principles involved is contained in Meade,[4] and the analysis here owes much to that approach.

A full social dividend scheme is an attractively simple proposal which would replace all taxes and benefits by cash payments to individuals, based only on citizenship, and by a single tax rate on all income. All contingent benefits would therefore be abolished. This idea provides the thrust behind the proposals of Rhys Williams and Parker, and those of Vince. The disadvantage of such a scheme is evident from the discussion in the preceding section. Either the cash payments are extremely low, or the tax rates required to finance them are extremely high, or both.

This is evident from the specific numbers suggested by Vince and Parker. Vince's personal tax credit is £21 per week at 1983 prices, and the tax rate required is 44 per cent. Parker's personal basic income for an individual is £17 per week (in 1981), and the associated tax rate 50 per cent (although this incorporates the employer's national insurance contribution). The impression given by these numbers is a rather optimistic one. Parker assumes that considerable additional revenue is derived from reductions in tax relief for such items as mortgage interest and pension contributions, so that the effective taxation increase is a good deal larger than suggested. More importantly, tentative estimates suggest that both schemes would, as presented, involve a large net revenue cost; there are a number of difficulties in the procedure used by both studies to estimate tax revenue from national accounts. It therefore follows that the tax rates required to achieve revenue neutrality would be somewhat higher than suggested.

Nor is this observation entirely surprising. Consider Figure 3.4 which shows, in line AB, an income-related benefit which is withdrawn at 100 per cent of other income; with no other income, you receive benefit of A, with income of B you receive no benefit. Total benefit payment is OAB. The tax rate between O and B is 100 per cent, and those with incomes above B are unaffected. Now suppose we replace the income-related benefit by a social dividend. Everyone gets a flat amount of *C*, and total payment is *OCDE*. *C* has to be quite low if total payment – and therefore the tax rate required to raise the revenue – is similar to that with an income-related benefit. But now those with no other income are only given *C*. If we want to pay *A* to them, total benefit rises to *OAFE*, and the required tax rate rises accordingly. A full social dividend is a very expensive way of helping the poor; it is no accident that the benefits which we seek to replace are already highly income-related.

A way of ameliorating this difficulty is suggested by Meade, and is described as a two-tier social dividend. This introduces some contingent benefit, so that those whose incomes are likely to be very low obtain more than the basic income or tax credit. This device is used by both Vince and Parker. Vince introduces a non-earner credit of £45 per week. Parker is much less generous, but offers contingent credits for old age of up to £15 per week, other contingent credits for pregnancy, invalidity, and 'home care', and a restricted housing benefit.

An alternative response is to adjust the scheme in the direction of a 'modified social dividend'. This imposes a much higher rate of tax on the first tranche of income than on later earnings. This is the method adopted by Clark[5] and is a common feature of negative income tax proposals. Its disadvantages are well summarised by Meade; it remains ungenerous to poor households and aggravates work disincentives in this area, but it typically does so in an area in which there are relatively few households.

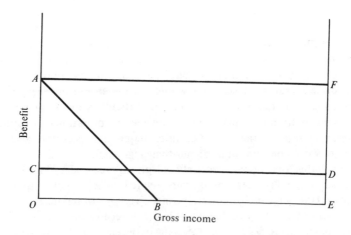

Fig. 3.4 Alternative ways of paying benefits

The reality is that a cost-effective approach to social security reform requires that the pure social dividend concept be modified in both these directions. The major advantage of the two-tier social dividend is that it enables us to give adequate support to those who are in contingencies — such as unemployment or old age — which carry a high risk of poverty, without the high marginal tax rates across the board which are inevitable if these levels of provision are to be made for the population as a whole. The advantage of the modified social dividend is that it enables us to reduce marginal rates of tax in areas of the distribution which are relatively dense, at the price of higher ones where relatively few families are to be found. The proposals which we put forward in Chapter 4 do both these things; this reflects the fact that they are done in the social security system as it stands today. In Chapter 5 we go beyond this and pursue the model of both contingent and income-related benefits as the normal model of a social benefit. We show how this can achieve greater efficiency in the achievement of the objectives of social security than can either the existing system or these previously proposed reforms.

Integrating tax and social security

Our objective, then, is to find a flexible and efficient mechanism for delivering benefits which reflect both individual circumstances and individual incomes. Since the direct tax system attempts to impose levies which reflect both individual circumstances and individual incomes, the case for bringing the tax and benefit systems together is a strong one. It is easy to see why they have grown up apart. Fifty years ago, very few people both paid taxes and received benefits. Now many benefit recipients are in this position. Although such integration sounds ambitious, time and technology are very much on its side. The price of storing, processing, and retrieving information is now unbelievably lower than it was when the main elements of our present tax and benefit systems were devised. The DHSS, Inland Revenue, and local authorities are large-scale employers of the kind of medium-grade clerical labour which the future will not require. Yet although technological changes have had some — inadequate — influence on how things are done, they have had virtually no influence as yet on what it is that is done. Calculation will continue to become cheaper, and the exercise of judgement will continue to grow more costly.

In seeking administrative reforms, there is no need to be frightened of proposals which are more demanding in terms of calculation and data processing than the present system. At the same time we should be seeking to standardise procedures, increase automaticity, and reduce discretion — in effect, to economise on those operations which require people rather than machines. We are confident that with efficient management, the kinds of arrangement we describe in the following pages could be operated with a substantial reduction in the number of staff currently employed in administering the present range of taxes and benefits. This does not mean that we are advocating a technological nightmare in which all needs are met by an inhuman computer. Rather, we should seek to employ people in the kinds of job that humans will always do better than computers — making judgements and dispensing help and advice to claimants and taxpayers.

The proposals in this book were designed with an intention of using the latest technology to implement them. If, for some reason, that technology were not available, or not available quickly, this does not mean that the proposals are unworkable. With imagination, we are confident that the structure proposed here could be administered under the administrative practices of the DHSS and the Inland Revenue, although this would be considerably less efficient than if modern technology were to be used.

The idea of achieving a closer integration of the tax and social security systems is not new. In our judgment, the most important recent intellectual contribution to the analysis of social security reform is the concept of the 'tax credit'. The idea behind it is that a contingent benefit can be paid to most of the population, not as a cash sum, but as an allowance through the tax system. The consequence is that the interaction of tax and social security can become more rational and more transparent. The idea of the tax credit is due to Lord Cockfield; it formed the basis of a scheme put forward in a Green Paper[6] in 1972 and was subsequently the subject of a select committee investigation.[7]

Tax credits and benefit credits

At present, the information provided in a tax return allows the Inland Revenue to compute the allowances due to any taxpayer. A coding, based on these allowances, is then used to determine the amount deducted from his pay each week or month. With tax allowances replaced by tax credits, precisely the same administrative procedures could be used to calculate the credits due to a taxpayer, and this is what would have happened under the Cockfield scheme. We also envisage that these administrative procedures would be used to compute benefit credits. It is these benefit credits, which would replace the major social security benefits (such as housing benefit and FIS) given to the working poor, which are at the centre of our proposed reforms.

How would a benefit credit work? Both tax credits and benefit credits are lump-sum payments which depend on the particular circumstances of the household – marital and working status, number of children, housing costs, etc. Both of them are reduced in amount as income increases, under a schedule which is prescribed for that group of taxes or benefits: by a tax schedule for income tax, by a withdrawal rate for benefits. The difference between a tax credit and a benefit credit is a simple one. A tax credit can reduce your tax liability, but the most it can do is to extinguish it. If your income is very low, the tax you pay will fall correspondingly; but however high your tax credit and low your income, the smallest amount you can pay in tax is zero. A benefit credit works in just the opposite way. However high your income is, the most it can do is to extinguish your benefit credit. The minimum you can receive is zero, regardless of how low your benefit credit may be and how high your income.

The following example may help to clarify the scheme. Suppose the marginal rate of tax is 30 per cent, and a household is entitled to a tax credit of £24. If its income is less than £80 its tax liability (30 per cent of £80) will be extinguished by its tax credit. Suppose that the benefit credit is £24 with a marginal rate of withdrawal of 30 per cent: the effect is that someone with no other income would get £24; someone earning £30 would be paid £15 (£24 less 30 per cent of £30). Someone on £80 would neither pay nor receive: the tax liability would be eliminated by the tax credit, and the benefit credit would be eliminated by his income.

Clearly, there is no special reason why the tax and benefit credits have to be structured in the same way. If the benefit credit were £40, with a marginal withdrawal rate of 50 per cent, then everyone with an income above £80 – in the paying rather than the receiving range – would be unaffected. Everyone below this would be better off than in the earlier example, but the price would be a higher effective rate of tax on people in this range.

We have structured these particular examples so that there is no overlap between tax credits and benefit credits. This need not be the case. If the benefit credit were £50, and the marginal withdrawal rate remained at 50 per cent, then everyone with an income below £100 would receive some benefit credit. The break-even point is around £93, at which income a household would both receive a benefit credit of £3 and pay the same amount in tax.

There is at first sight something odd about an overlap of this kind, and for many critics the existence of households which both pay and receive is in itself a disadvantage of the present system. One reason for permitting such a possibility is that it exists within the present system, and if we are to reproduce the effects of that system we need to allow for it. There are, however, reasons for thinking that such an overlap might be described as the best available balance between conflicting objectives. The principal reason is that it may well be desirable to award benefit credits on a basis which discriminates more carefully between types of household than is appropriate for tax credits. Certainly, it is true at the moment that benefit calculations are based on a more elaborate analysis of household circumstances, and it is likely to remain the case that efficiently relating benefits to needs requires information, about housing costs for example, which would not be thought relevant to the assessment of tax liability. If this possibility is accepted then it follows that benefit credits and tax credits will be awarded on somewhat different criteria and that overlap cannot be excluded.

The scheme which has in the past come closest to implementation is the 1972 tax credit proposals. These are described in some detail in the appendix to this chapter. There were two major reasons why the 1972 proposals were criticised. The first was that, because income tax assessment was to be weekly, it was necessary to have a single basic rate of tax for all taxpayers. This in turn led directly to the second criticism, which was mainly directed at the inability of a tax credit scheme to replace the present wide basic-rate band by a more elaborately graduated structure of marginal rates. Since we see no great advantage in such a structure, we are not especially concerned by this restriction (although the proposals put forward here remove it). A more serious criticism is that a single-rate tax system allows benefits to be withdrawn only very slowly from medium-income families. This limits the range of benefits which can be incorporated into the system, and under the 1972 tax credit scheme most means-tested benefits would have been retained, with all their implied complexity. The scheme proposed here incorporates a dual-rate system. The addition of a second rate to the structure is sufficient to overcome the major problems which emerged in the system proposed in 1972.

Appendix: The 1972 tax credit scheme

In the Budget speech of March 1972, the Chancellor (Anthony Barber) announced that the Government was considering a scheme for tax credits designed by his special advisor on taxation, Sir Arthur (now Lord) Cockfield. The scheme, which the Chancellor described as representing 'The most radical reform . . . of the PAYE and Social Security system for a quarter of a century' was described in detail in a Green Paper.[8] This explained the main principles of the scheme and described its objectives as follows:

(i) 'to simplify and reform the whole system of personal tax collection' and

(ii) 'to improve the system of income support for poor people'.

The scheme included a radical change to the way income tax was administered and a limited integration with benefits. PAYE was to be abolished and replaced by a non-cumulative system in which tax liability was based on weekly, rather than annual, income. Personal allowances were to be replaced by tax credits of greater value, the addition reflecting the values of family allowances. The illustrative figures given in the Green Paper were as follows:

	Green Paper 'illustrative figures'	1973/4 value of allowance to basic-rate taxpayers
Single person	£4 p.w.	£3.43 p.w.
Married man or single parent	£6 p.w.	£4.47 p.w.
For each child	£2 p.w.	£1.36 p.w. (average) plus family allowance of £0.90 p.w. for second child and £1.00 p.w. for subsequent children, less clawback of £0.34 per eligible child.

If an individual's income were such that his tax liability at the basic rate (then 30 per cent) on all his income were less than his tax credit, then under the scheme he would receive a payment in his pay-packet equal to the amount of the discrepancy. Someone with no other income would receive the full tax credit. All the national insurance benefits were retained as a separate system, as were national insurance contributions, the only change being that short-term unemployment and sickness-benefits were to be made taxable. Supplementary benefit and the other means-tested benefits were to be retained. The only benefits which were to be incorporated into the new system were family allowances and, for those covered by the scheme, FIS. The self-employed, those with low earnings (below one-quarter of male average industrial earnings), and those receiving supplementary benefit but not national insurance benefits (for example the long-term unemployed) — at the time totalling about 10 per cent of the population — were excluded from the scheme.

The tax credit scheme was examined by a select committee which was appointed in December 1972 and reported in July 1973.[9] The majority recommended acceptance of the scheme with certain modifications, although two minority reports[10] disagreed. A major modification was that, whereas the Green Paper intended child credit payments to be made to the husband of a couple, the select committee, after having received numerous representations[11] on the subject, recommended that payments be made to the wife at the Post Office and that the payment should be universal, covering those not included in the scheme as well. This recommendation was accepted by the Government.

On 19 July 1973 the Chancellor of the Exchequer claimed that the new system would 'represent a major social advance'. However, a significant number of people disagreed with this view. An influential analysis carried out (for the IFS) by A.B. Atkinson[12] investigated the redistributive effects. It showed that the scheme would help those not then taking-up FIS, and would help the poorest pensioners, but at the expense of making pensioners with incomes a little above the supplementary benefit line, and those currently receiving FIS, much worse off. In addition, it would reduce the incomes of many unemployed families and still leave over two million households on supplementary benefit. The scheme was also criticised for leaving a large number of families with a marginal rate of tax of 49 per cent, and for failing to achieve other desirable redistributional goals. Perhaps the major criticism was the limited nature of its effects:

Despite the claims made for it, the Green Paper is a half-hearted document. It recognises the need for substantial transfer of resources to those with low incomes, but does not have the courage to say how this is to be financed. It is described as a radical reform, but it nowhere examines the structure of benefits to be provided to different groups, and the redistribution which would ensue is based on no coherent principles. It aims both to simplify the tax system and to improve income support, but fails to recognise that these objectives may well be in conflict. It acknowledges that means-tested benefits are ineffective, yet it offers no hope of going further than the abolition of FIS. It stresses the importance of the poverty trap, but leaves many families facing marginal tax rates of nearly 50%. Such a document does not appear the best foundation for social policy in the next quarter of a century.[13]

A second set of criticisms concerned its administrative infeasibility. Income tax assessment was to be moved from a weekly to an annual basis. This implied that those with fluctuating incomes would be treated very differently from equally well-placed individuals with stable incomes.

References and notes

1. A.B. Atkinson, *The Tax Credit Scheme and the Redistribution of Income*, London, Institute for Fiscal Studies (September 1973).
2. In Britain, the idea of 'social dividend' had its origins in the paper 'Something to look forward to' (MacDonald, 1943) by Lady Rhys Williams.
3. The principal proposals discussed here are those of Clark, Rhys Williams and Parker, Stewart, and Vince. The versions discussed are those submitted in evidence to the Treasury and Civil Service Select Committee 1983.
4. J.E. Meade, *The Structure and Reform of Direct Taxation* (report of Institute for Fiscal Studies committee under the chairmanship of J.E. Meade), London, Allen and Unwin (1978).
5. Clark, in Treasury and Civil Service Select Committee 1983, op. cit.

6. *Proposals for a Tax Credit System* (Green Paper), Cmnd. 5116, London, HMSO (1972).

7. Select Committee on Tax Credit, *Vol. I, Report and Proceedings of the Committee*, H.C. 341-I (1973).

8. *Proposals for a Tax Credit System*, op. cit.

9. Select Committee on Tax Credit, op. cit.

10. That of J. Barnett MP and R. Sheldon MP, which noted the lack of flexibility caused by a single rate of tax, and of Barbara Castle MP, which expressed concern that the proposals did very little for the poorest families.

11. See Select Committee on Tax Credit, op. cit.

12. Atkinson, op. cit.

13. Ibid., p. 85.

4

Structural Reforms

Is substantive integration of the tax and social security systems an administrative possibility, or simply a romantic dream? In Britain and elsewhere, the two systems grew up separately because they operated for essentially distinct groups of people. One class of individual paid taxes, and another received benefits. The two administrations developed in different buildings and in different styles. If it had been envisaged that one day most people would be both taxpayers and benefit recipients, usually at the same time, it is inconceivable that things would have developed this way. It will always be true that the technical side of personal taxation will require the special skills of trained inspectors. But most tax administration is not – now – of this kind. The clientele of the PAYE enquiry office overlaps extensively with that of the DHSS office. The school-leaver obtaining his first job, the newly redundant worker, the person planning to retire, the newly bereaved widow, will provide the same information and answer rather similar questions for both the Inland Revenue and the DHSS; and in neither place, nor anywhere else, will he or she find any comprehensive guidance on the range of financial relations between the individual and the state.

In the first part of this chapter, we consider how the concept of the benefit credit can be used to absorb the principal means-tested benefits into the framework of income tax. In the second part, we describe how such a scheme ought to be administered.

Benefit credits for working households

Benefit credits were defined in Chapter 3. A benefit credit is a payment, made in full if the household has no income and withdrawn through the tax system as income increases. Any particular component of benefit credit is described by the amount of the credit and the rate at which it is withdrawn. The specific rates of benefit credit which we use in this chapter have been chosen with some care. They are the result of extensive computer simulations which have been designed to establish those rates of benefit credit which minimise the gains or losses made by individual households relative to their present position. Our intention is to replicate as closely as possible the distribution of benefits in the existing system but with a much simpler administrative structure. It is important to stress that this approximation to the status quo is a feature of the system taken as a whole, rather than of each individual step in it.

Our objective is to transform the existing system into a group of tax credits, with corresponding tax rates on income, and benefit credits, with corresponding withdrawal rates on income. At current tax rates, the personal tax allowances are equivalent in value to tax credits of £10.30 per week for a single person and £16.13 for a married man. Their value to higher-rate taxpayers is rather greater. We reproduce this by raising the threshold at which higher rates of tax become payable by £2,795 per annum, the amount of the married man's allowance. This leaves single higher-rate taxpayers somewhat better off, but the number of people in this category is extremely small.

National insurance contributions become a flat-rate tax up to the upper earnings limit on income. A tax credit of £2.93 per week (9 per cent of £32.50) is provided, but this is available only to those with incomes below the lower earnings limit. This reproduces the current effect of the lower earnings limit, and continues the high marginal tax rate on those whose earnings barely exceed it. More substantive integration of tax and national insurance schedules is impossible without some significant redistribution. This is because the married man's allowance implies that couples are more favourably treated under income tax than by national insurance. We consider these issues further in Chapter 5.

If the head of a childless household is in work, housing benefit is the only major benefit to which that household is normally entitled. Housing benefit for such a household is calculated by reference to the relationship between household income less earnings disregards, and a needs allowance based on the size of the household. The amount of benefit payable is then calculated by taking 60 per cent of the rent and rates payable and increasing these figures by 25 per cent and 8 per cent respectively of the shortfall between income and needs allowance, or reducing them by 21 per cent and 7 per cent respectively of the excess of income over needs allowance. Payments of less than 20p per week in respect of rent and 10p in respect of rates are not made.

The relationship between housing benefit and income which this implies for a single person is shown by the solid line in Figure 4.1. The shape of the curve is initially flat, because no household can receive

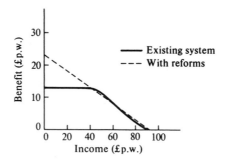

Fig. 4.1 Benefits and benefit credits for households without children

more than the whole of its rent and rates in housing benefit. Thereafter the slope reflects the rates at which benefit is withdrawn as income increases, varying as income is above or below the needs allowance.
The pattern shown is in fact rather oversimplified; this is because there
are separate minimum and maximum payments for the rent and rate
components of housing benefit. The position of the curve, and the
kinks in it, do of course vary for different households.

The broken line in Figure 4.1 replaces housing benefit by a general
benefit credit of £12.50 per week (for a single person) or £18 (for a
couple) plus 80 per cent of rent and rates, withdrawn at a rate of 25
per cent. This implies gains and losses for individual households, generally small, depending on income levels; very low-income households
tend to do well from the change, but this is not true in all cases. We
return later to a review of the overall pattern of gains and losses.

A couple with children could now expect to receive, if its income
was sufficiently low, additional benefits for children from family
income supplement (FIS) and from free school meals, and an addition
to its housing benefit.

FIS is also based on the difference between income, and on a needs
allowance, although all parameters of this calculation differ from those
which relate to housing benefit. The claimant then receives 50 per cent
of the shortfall thus calculated, subject to a maximum payment which
depends on the number of children in the family. Children in households receiving FIS are entitled to free school meals. These may also be
provided to others at the (now rarely exercised) discretion of the
local authority.

The solid line in Figure 4.2 shows the relationship between benefit
entitlement and income level which applies in this case. An upper limit
is set by the income level at which the maximum level of FIS is payable

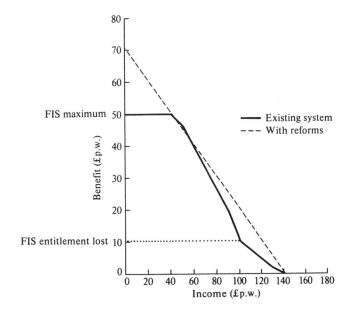

Fig. 4.2 Benefits and benefit credits for households with children

and at which rent and rate rebates are paid in full. As income increases, one or other benefit (generally FIS) is reduced, and at a somewhat higher level benefit receipts fall more sharply as both benefits start to be withdrawn. Benefit receipts drop sharply as entitlement to FIS disappears altogether and with it the right to free school meals. Thereafter, however, the effective marginal tax rate is lower as only housing benefit remains to be withdrawn.

Again, we drive the broken line in Figure 4.2 through this complicated pattern. The couple's benefit credit remains at £18 per week, but we provide an additional benefit credit of £30.35 for the first child and £5.50 for each additional child in the family. These rather extraordinary figures reflect the existing structure of FIS. Because any entitlement is conditional on there being at least one child in the family, the implied subsidy to the first child in a household is very large and that for subsequent children relatively small.

If there is a second earner in the household, the wife will receive a tax credit of £10.30, equivalent to the current wife's earned income relief. In addition, the wife's income will be added to that of her husband for the purpose of assessing entitlement to benefit credit. We later consider further the administrative procedures by which this might be achieved.

(£p.w., assumed rent £18,
rates £5.85, single-earner
not contracted-out of SERPS)

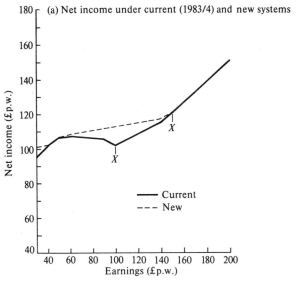

(a) Net income under current (1983/4) and new systems

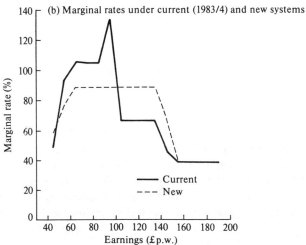

(b) Marginal rates under current (1983/4) and new systems

Fig. 4.3   Net incomes and marginal rates for couples with two children, head working

In Figure 4.3 we show how a particular household might be affected by these changes. We have introduced a slight gradient into the poverty

TABLE 4.1
The new system for working families

Type of family	Average net incomes*			% with new income			
	Average existing (1983/4) net income (£ p.w.)	Average new net income (£ p.w.)	Over 3% less	1–3% less	Within 1% of present	1–3% more	Over 3% more†
Single	109.16	109.50	3	5	79	9	4
Single-earner couples							
0-child couple	145.58	145.98	–	6	82	7	5
1-child couple	155.94	156.23	–	2	90	4	5
2-child couple	161.81	162.65	–	2	81	6	11
3-child couple	167.14	168.55	–	1	77	6	16
4-child couple	185.80	187.46	3	14	54	11	19
Two-earner couples							
0-child couple	192.18	192.42	–	1	94	2	3
1-child couple	187.63	188.33	–	1	93	3	3
2-child couple	191.29	191.66	–	2	94	2	2
3-child couple	212.31	212.89	–	–	91	2	7
4-child couple	181.55	183.23	–	–	76	12	12
Overall	169.28	169.77	–	2	88	5	5

Notes: *Incomes here are based on entitlement to benefit rather than receipt – in some cases, non take-up of entitlement will mean incomes received are lower.
†These are the families who were in the 'poverty trap'.

plateau shown in Figure 4.3(a). This means that it is now impossible for anyone to be worse off as a result of an increase in their earnings. As Figure 4.3(b) shows, the present rather complex pattern

TABLE 4.2A
The new system: marginal rates
(%)

	Av Mr	Existing (1983/4)					
		> 100 (a)	> 80 (b)	> 60 (c)	> 40 (d)	> 30 (e)	<= 30 (f)
Single	40.3	–	–	9	15	63	13
Single-earner couples							
0-child couple	38.4	–	–	7	11	60	22
1-child couple	38.8	2	–	5	10	57	26
2-child couple	41.6	3	2	7	9	55	24
3-child couple	45.7	5	5	10	9	53	19
4-child couple	55.1	14	11	8	16	38	14
Two-earner couples							
0-child couple	36.3	–	–	1	3	79	17
1-child couple	36.8	–	–	2	5	74	19
2-child couple	37.4	–	–	2	7	73	18
3-child couple	37.3	–	1	2	9	62	26
4-child couple	42.2	6	–	–	18	71	6
Overall	38.7	1	1	4	8	67	19

Notes: (i) Marginal rates in the existing system are caused by:
    (a) Income tax, NI, FIS, and rent and rate rebates. In some cases they exceed even 105 per cent because passport benefits are withdrawn.
    (b) Income tax, NI, and FIS.
    (c) Income tax, NI, and rent and rate rebates.
    (d) Income tax and NI. Some higher-rate taxpayers included.
    (e) Income tax alone.
    (f) NI alone, or no tax, or no NI (below income tax threshold or NI floor).

TABLE 4.2B
The new system: marginal rates
(%)

Av Mr	> 100	New > 80 (a)	> 60 (b)	> 40 (c)	> 30 (c)	<= 30 (d)
41.4	–	–	19	–	68	13
38.9	–	–	13	1	64	22
39.8	–	9	–	–	64	27
44.0	–	16	–	1	59	24
50.9	–	28	–	3	50	19
61.4	–	49	–	5	32	14
36.7	–	–	2	1	80	17
37.4	–	2	–	3	77	18
37.6	–	3	–	3	77	17
39.2	–	5	2	2	65	26
46.4	–	18	–	6	71	5
39.9	–	5	4	1	70	20

Notes: (ii) Marginal rates in the new system are caused by:
 (a) Those receiving net benefit credit and paying tax and NI.
 (b) Families receiving net benefit credit but with incomes below the tax threshold.
 (c) Those with no net benefit credit but paying income tax – including higher-rate taxpayers.
 (d) Below tax threshold but receiving partial net benefit.
 (iii) Marginal rates in this table are those applicable to the principal earner.

of marginal rates is simplified and an upper limit imposed to the level which they can reach. However, there are two disadvantages. The first is that the marginal rate of tax faced by poor families remains very high, at 89 per cent in many cases. The second is that we have achieved a reduction to this level principally by extending the range over which benefit credit is payable. Although households in the range XX in Figure 4.3(a) are now slightly better off, they face a higher marginal tax rate as a result of the withdrawal of benefit. This difficulty reflects the fundamentally intractable nature of major amelioration of the poverty trap, which we described on page 71; we must either make poor households poorer, or extend high marginal tax rates into more densely populated regions of the income distribution.

These results are reflected in the pattern of marginal rates of tax which we describe in Table 4.1. No households now have marginal rates over 100 per cent; but there is an increase in the number who face rates over 60 per cent. The average of marginal rates of tax for the population of working households taken as a whole rises slightly, from its present 38.7 per cent to 39.9 per cent. In Table 4.2 we present the distribution of gains and losses to individual households which result from the wholesale substitution of simplified benefit credits for the existing pattern of housing and child benefits with its variable tapers, needs allowances, and disregards. 88 per cent of households have net incomes which are within 1 per cent of their present entitlement. There is a small net revenue cost to the rates of benefit credit described earlier. The gainers are principally low-income households in the poverty trap.

Single-parent families

The benefit position of single-parent families is considerably more complex than that of other kinds of household. The principal reason is that they have the choice of two alternative regimes. One is based on a modified supplementary benefit (SB) scale. The other possibility is that they can opt to be treated in the same way as other households, and receive housing benefit and FIS. The head of the household can, if he or she understands the system sufficiently, or is well advised, select that combination of benefits which is most advantageous.

If supplementary benefit is chosen, the household can earn £4 per week before suffering any loss of benefit, the next £20 of income reduces benefit by 50p for each £1 of earnings, and thereafter entitlement is decreased £ for £. If housing benefit/FIS is preferred, the rules are similar to those for two-parent households.

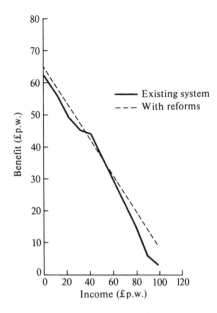

Fig. 4.4 Benefits and benefit credits for one-parent families

The pattern which results is shown in Figure 4.4 which illustrates benefit receipts under the two different systems. The advantageous choice under the present system is shown by the solid line. Again, we attempt to drive a simple linear schedule through these complexities. The appropriate benefit credit regime is influenced by the present structure of SB payments. It therefore includes 100 per cent, rather than 80 per cent, of housing costs. In addition, a one-parent addition of £7 is required, on top of the single benefit credit of £12.50 which is given more generally. Child payments are £9.15 per week for children under 11 and £13.70 for others. This is based on the more balanced SB scale rather than on the FIS regime with its emphasis on provision for the first child.

It is difficult to mirror at all precisely the existing hodgepodge of benefits to this category of households. This difficulty is aggravated by the fact that one-parent families are a very heterogeneous group. A minority — but only a minority — are young mothers with a single child, living with parents. There are many older parents with dead or divorced spouses. Some of this group have high incomes; many are owner-occupiers.

The changes to the tax system follow closely the pattern applied to

TABLE 4.3
*Distributional and marginal rate effects of the new system
on one-parent families*

Distributional effects		
Average net incomes		
Under existing (1983/4 system)	£100.84 p.w.	
Under new system	£100.53 p.w.	
Percentage with new incomes		
Over 3% lower	15	
1–3% lower	8	
Within 1%	31	
1–3% higher	22	
Over 3% higher	25	
Marginal rates	Under Existing (1983/4) system	Under new system
Average marginal rate	56.9%	55.8%
Distribution of marginal rates (%)		
100% and over	5	–
80–100%	9	20
60– 80%	11	–
40– 60%	62	63
30– 40%	8	13
Below 30%	5	5

households generally. At present, a single parent receives both a single person's allowance and an 'additional personal allowance'. The value of the two taken together is equal to the married man's allowance. Both of these allowances would become tax credits, and the extension of the basic rate band leaves the tax position of the small number of single-parent families liable to higher-rate tax unaffected.

As Table 4.3 shows, a substantial majority of single-parent families would benefit from these changes, although 15 per cent of all such households would lose by more than 3 per cent of their net income. The overall effect is more or less revenue neutral. Households in this category inevitably face high effective marginal rates of tax because they are so likely to be dependent on benefits. At present, 5 per cent are confronted by rates of tax in excess of 100 per cent, and the average for all households is 56.9 per cent. Our modifications eliminate rates over 100 per cent and reduce the average marginal rates slightly to 55.8 per cent.

Pensioners

The structure of benefits and allowances for pensioners is a particularly striking example of the irrational complexities of piecemeal development. A pensioner, or pensioner couple, receives a basic national insurance benefit plus, in some cases, an earnings-related component resulting either from the old graduated pension scheme or from the new state earnings-related scheme. If pensioners have no resources significantly beyond the national insurance pension, they may also be entitled to a supplementary pension. They will also be entitled to housing benefit. There are two alternative formulae for housing benefit. One pays rent and rates in full but imposes a 100 per cent marginal tax rate on other income. The other corresponds in structure, although not in detail, to the housing benefit paid to working families. The benefit offers a payment of a proportion of rent and rates, increased or reduced by a variable fraction of the difference between actual income and a needs allowance. All households should receive the higher of the two amounts so calculated. In addition, pensioners under 70 are subject to an earnings rule by which their pension is reduced by reference to their earnings (although not to their income from other sources). There is an enhanced tax allowance for couples where one partner is over 65, with a taper which phases this out from those whose income, including benefits, exceeds £7,600 per year.

The relationship between benefit (and the income which this implies) is shown by the bold line in Figure 4.5. It is difficult to reproduce this structure with any simpler system, and hard to imagine why anyone would want to. Once again, we drive a simple linear schedule through the current system. The benefit credit is determined by the relationship between supplementary benefit and the basic pension and the relevant housing benefit structure. We continue to pay the state pension on the same basis, provide a very small benefit credit of 20p or 40p per week to mirror the excess of the long-term SB scale over the pension, and a further benefit credit of 100 per cent of housing costs. The benefit credit is withdrawn at a rate of 20 per cent — somewhere between the withdrawal rate of housing benefit for a pensioner paying both rent and rates, and that faced by a pensioner paying rates alone. As with other households, the tax allowances now available are converted into tax credits. For the present, the age allowance continues to be withdrawn above £7,600.

As illustrated by Figure 4.5, the structure of benefit receipt faced by pensioners is bizarre, particularly at low levels of income, and most pensioners have very low levels of income. For this reason, the new

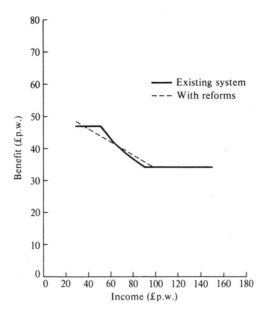

Fig. 4.5 Benefits and benefit credits for pensioners

system fails to reproduce the existing net income distribution as success-fully for pensioners as for other types of household. While we have matched the net incomes of the current system for pensioners with no income other than the basic state pension, it is impossible to reproduce the structure for those with a little extra income without falling prey to the complexities that we are trying to avoid. The structure of marginal rates faced by pensioners is little changed (see Table 4.4).

Unemployment and sickness

An unemployed person with an appropriate contribution record is currently entitled to unemployment benefit, for himself and any dependents, during the first twelve months of unemployment. While receiving unemployment benefit he will also be eligible for supplementary benefit and/or housing benefit. Unemployment benefit is paid without regard to past or current income. Supplementary benefit is withdrawn £ for £ once a very small disregard is reached. Depending on the precise circumstances of the household, an increase in income may have no effect on housing benefit; or it may lead to it

TABLE 4.4
Distributional and marginal rate effects of the new system on pensioners

Distributional effects

Type of family	Average net incomes		% with new income				
	Average existing (1983/4) net income (£ p.w.)	Average new net income (£ p.w.)	Over 3% less	1–3% less	Within 1% of present	1–3% more	Over 3% more
Single pensioner	54.20	54.57	4	16	64	7	9
Couple pensioner	91.58	92.78	1	13	52	24	10

Marginal rates (%)

Existing (1983/4)

	Average marginal rate	> 100	> 80	> 60	> 40	> 30	<= 30
Single pensioner	14.3	–	–	4	5	17	74
Couple pensioner	21.8	–	–	3	8	26	63

New

	Average marginal rate	> 100	> 80	> 60	> 40	> 30	<= 30
Single pensioner	29.0	–	–	–	21	4	75
Couple pensioner	33.5	–	–	–	28	13	58

being reduced at a rate of between 7 per cent and 33 per cent, as applies to working households; or it may be reduced £ for £. Most people in the UK are now entitled to statutory sick pay (SSP) if they are unfit for work. This benefit is payable by the employer, who can deduct the cost from his national insurance contributions, and lasts for a maximum of eight weeks in any one tax year.

SSP is set at a level related to previous earnings. When SSP eligibility is exhausted, claimants move on to national insurance sickness benefit. This is a flat-rate benefit independent of previous earnings, and is paid directly by the DHSS. After twenty-eight weeks of entitlement to either SSP and sickness benefit, or to sickness benefit alone, claimants become eligible for invalidity pension, a flat rate national insurance benefit slightly more generous than sickness benefit. Throughout the period of sickness, claimants may be entitled to supplementary benefit and housing benefit in addition to their sickness-related benefits, depending on the amount of these benefits and the other resources which they have. This dreadful mess is a tribute to the havoc which politicians' over-zealous response to interest group pressures can create.

The sort of benefit schedule implied is illustrated in Figure 4.6. We would propose to continue to pay the contingent benefits, such as

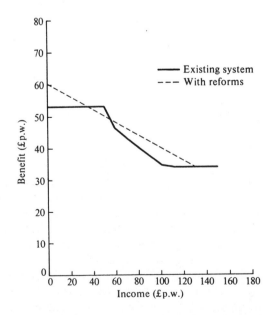

Fig. 4.6 Benefits and benefit credits for the unemployed and sick

unemployment or sickness benefit, as a non-withdrawable benefit, as in the case of retirement pension. A benefit credit for the sick or un-employed would provide 100 per cent of housing costs, and child credits as benefit credits would be withdrawn on other income at a rate of 50 per cent for families with children and 25 per cent for those without. The child credits here are the relevant SB scales. This com-bination of credits and withdrawal rates reproduces quite well benefit receipts under the current system.

Administering the system

At present, the Inland Revenue collects information on the income of taxpayers, whether they are married, their employment status (are they retired or unemployed?), and their expenditure on mortgage interest. Until 1979 it also kept records of the number of children dependent on a taxpayer, but now no longer normally does so. A local authority administering housing benefit obtains details of housing costs, of income over a five-week period, and of the marital status and number of children of the applicant. The DHSS bases its payment of national insurance benefits on employment status, marital status, number of children, and its records of past contributions. Entitlement to supplementary benefit depends on employment status, marital status, number of children, and current income. FIS is determined by income over a five-week period, employment status, and number of children.

Payment of tax, and entitlement to the principal social security benefits, therefore depend on the following factors: income; employ-ment status; marital status; number of children; housing costs. At present, most of this information is collected from most households by someone; for many households, much of it is collected by more than one agency; but not all of it is collected by any single agency from anyone. It is obvious that there is scope for rationalisation. We propose that responsibility for obtaining and processing this inform-ation should rest with a single organisation, based on the PAYE oper-ation of the Inland Revenue and the benefit administration activities of the DHSS. The records for an individual would be maintained by reference to his place of residence, and the local office of the joint organisation would be the normal point of contact with the tax or benefit system for the average person. Schedule D assessment of the self-employed, and the management of tax affairs of those with high or complex incomes, would remain the province of specialist tax offices; these would have a role and workload similar to that of tax offices before the Second World War. In conjunction with these administrative changes, we look for a substantive integration in which income tax and national insurance contributions are amalgamated, tax allowances are transformed into tax credits, and the principal social security benefits paid to those in work are replaced by benefit credits implemented through the tax system.

In what follows, we are not proposing a specific timetable for reform, which we do not doubt would be a gradual process. Nor are we spelling out every administrative detail. It is necessary that objectives should be agreed and understood before these steps can usefully be undertaken. But it is incumbent on us to provide enough discussion of administrative issues to identify the principal problems and suggest lines of solution to them.

The Inland Revenue currently undertakes two main activities for a PAYE taxpayer. It sends out a return of income form, processes the information contained in it, and makes an assessment of liability to tax in the year that has passed. For a high proportion of taxpayers with simple affairs, this process is frequently dispensed with, on the assumption that tax has been correctly charged by deductions under PAYE. A majority of taxpayers receive a return only once every five years. The second task is that of issuing a 'notice of coding', at least annually, which states the allowances to which the taxpayer is entitled and forms the basis of the tax deductions which are made from his wages or salary each week or each month by his employer. This notice of coding is based on the information supplied in the taxpayer's return of income in the current, or an earlier, year, together with any changes — such as marriage — which he may have notified to the Inland Revenue.

In the following pages, we describe how these procedures might be extended to enable them to be applied not only to tax allowances, but also to calculate the tax and benefit credits due to individuals or households and to construct procedures by which these could be paid to the working population through their pay-packets. Not all the changes we propose are actually specific or necessary consequences of our reforms — some are simply a necessary part of streamlining and modernising the system. They follow closely a number of the suggestions made by the Keith Committee[1] on the enforcement powers of the Revenue departments for the reform of income tax administration.

All taxpayers would be required to make an annual return of income to the Inland Revenue. The obligation to file a return would be similar in form to the existing obligation which requires those liable to tax to declare their income. In practice, forms would be sent to most taxpayers but would also be available at post offices and tax benefit offices. Anyone else could submit a return, and people who would be entitled to benefits but who were not liable for tax would clearly find it advantageous to do so. We do not, however, envisage that compulsion would extend beyond those liable for tax, and to this extent potential beneficiaries could escape the net and some problems of take-up of benefit would remain. Unless we are prepared to imprison confused old ladies for failing to claim rate rebates, there is no income transfer mechanism which can escape this problem.

Payers of income would be required to notify both the Inland Revenue and the taxpayer of the amount of income which had been paid in the course of a fiscal year. This obligation would fall broadly on those who are now required to report income and withhold tax, and would involve a form similar to the P60 now provided to employees. For dividends and interest, a redesigned tax voucher would serve the purpose. Taxpayers would simply transfer to their annual return the amount of taxable income, and tax withheld, recorded on these forms. As now, they would also be required to report any other income which they had received.

The principal change to the tax return form is that it would also establish the information needed to determine benefit entitlement. It would therefore be necessary to give details of marital status (as now), and of dependent children (which has not been required since 1979 but is, of course, supplied separately for child benefit). Details of housing costs pose more difficulty. Information would be required on the amount of rent paid in the previous year and expected to be paid in the coming year. For local authorities, housing associations, and other public-sector landlords — who now own most rented accommodation in Britain — this is straightforward. Private landlords pose more problems. A tenant would have a right to demand a statement from his landlord of the amount of rent he had paid in the previous twelve months — a procedure which might, incidentally, aid enforcement of income tax on rent — akin to his present right to a rent book. As with this latter right, the procedure could not be wholly effective and would inevitably depend on the honesty of taxpayers, aided by the possibility of prosecution for supplying wilfully false information. Local authorities would supply with their rate demands a statement of rates paid and to be paid, which would be in a form which could be transferred directly to tax returns.

It would be absurd to seek information about housing costs from the millions of households whose net tax payments would not be affected by it (although we note that the existing tax return form requests information, such as receipt of building society interest, which necessitates a response from most taxpayers but is normally irrelevant to their liability). We therefore propose that the guidance notes should indicate an income level above which it is unlikely that any housing benefit credit would be payable, and that taxpayers should have the option of ticking a box indicating that they did not wish to claim any housing benefit credit. An important issue is to define exactly who is entitled to claim in respect of any particular payment of rent or rates. This leads immediately to the problem of defining the tax and benefit unit, which we consider further in Appendix B to this chapter.

There would be a time limit for the completion of the annual return and this would be enforced by automatic, although initially modest, penalties for those liable to tax. We envisage that this limit would not be more than three months after the end of the fiscal year. Although these procedures are common practice in other countries, we recognise that habits in the UK are such that they would raise problems for the self-employed if adopted here. We propose that, for the self-employed, the existing preceding-year basis would be transformed into a system of preliminary assessment, and this would allow a more leisurely submission of full accounts.

At this stage, processing of the annual return would simply consist of a mechanical appraisal for obvious errors of entry or transcription. There would be no assessment of the substance or veracity of the data at this stage. The computer would automatically send to the taxpayer a magnetic coding card which would replace existing notices of coding and record his tax and benefit credits. A printed statement of the information on which this calculation had been based would also be supplied. The computer would also check tax due against tax paid, and issue refunds or adjust the coding information for previous underpayments. The card would be effective until exchanged for a new card, with a maximum period of validity of around twelve months. An employee would take the coding card to his employer, and it would then form the basis of his PAYE deductions. An unemployed person would lodge it with the DHSS, where it would be used to calculate and issue his benefit entitlement. A retired person would be able either to use it at a post office or to lodge it with the DHSS under a procedure similar to that for the unemployed. If circumstances changed — for example marriage, children, or a large change in rent — a new card would be issued valid for subsequent weeks, and the same would happen if a card were lost.

The simplest kind of card would simply contain magnetically coded information about its user, similar to those supplied by banks and building societies for use in automated teller machines (ATMs). It would seem desirable that each use of the card should automatically cancel an entry for the appropriate week of the fiscal year, similar to the cancelling of units on a British Telecom card. There is no reason why long-term benefit recipients should not be able to use these cards to draw benefit from ATMs, which might be those of banks or building societies, or specific to the Inland Revenue/Department of Health and Social Security. A more sophisticated development could involve the use of a 'smart card', which contains its own memory; this would enable the card to maintain a continuous record of tax credits or benefit credits already paid, and facilitate the operation of cumulative PAYE. Although this technology must sound fanciful to those familiar with current Inland Revenue and DHSS procedures, it is already in regular use by unsophisticated customers and employees of organisations in the private sector.

Employers would be issued by the Inland Revenue with card-reading microprocessor units. For small employers, these would compute the tax due from or net benefit payable to each employee and the aggregate tax due from the employer. Anyone who has ever seen a set of volumes of PAYE tables will realise that this change is long overdue, whether or not the full set of reforms we are describing are implemented. For those with computerised payroll systems, approved units would be available to transfer the coded information into a format compatible with their procedures. It is not intended that the coding information could be read directly by employers; but although it would not be readily accessible to office busybodies, it is probably unrealistic to think that it would be possible to maintain confidentiality if an employer was anxious to obtain the information. This is partly a matter for data protection legislation — urgently needed in any event.

These procedures imply a peak workload in the first third of the fiscal year. The remainder of the period would be used for checking the substance of the information provided. In the US, the Internal Revenue Service has the power to select taxpayers randomly for audit; although we see advantages in such powers existing here, we do not think they would be necessary for effective enforcement. There is, of course, nothing to stop an inspector selecting a return at random for his more careful — internal — perusal, and we envisage that a selection of returns would be considered in this way, some chosen arbitrarily, some selected by the computer as displaying suspicious features. Where further enquiry seemed appropriate, supporting or additional information would be sought from the taxpayer. A relatively automatic penalty system would operate in the case of incorrect returns, perhaps along the lines favoured by the Keith Committee. If a particular taxpayer's case had not been selected for further scrutiny after a period of time had elapsed, or if such scrutiny had been completed, he would be notified that his return for the year in question had now been accepted. Such acceptance would have the same status as a current assessment, and would imply that the affairs of that year would only be reopened if error or fraud were subsequently 'discovered'. Existing procedures for resolving cases of dispute would remain unchanged.

Appendix A: Cumulation and non-cumulation

An important and complex issue in tax and benefit administration concerns the extent to which payments and receipts are cumulative or non-cumulative. Although the problem is a somewhat technical one, it is fundamental to the design of administration and important to the effect on incentives. A mechanism is cumulative if each weekly calculation takes account of experience in previous weeks; non-cumulative if successive weekly calculations are independent.

The available range of possibilities and combinations of possibilities is very large. First, liability may be cumulative or non-cumulative, while payments may independently be cumulative or non-cumulative. The British income tax system has cumulative liability and cumulative payment. Liability is based on annual income, and each week's tax deductions take account of the income and allowances received in previous weeks. National insurance contributions are an example of non-cumulative liability and non-cumulative payment. Each week's payment is based on the week's income. Moreover, so too is liability: even if average income over a year is such that there is no liability for any payment, payment is still required if income in any week of the year exceeds the lower earnings limit.

In the United States, income tax liability is cumulative but payment is non-cumulative. Tax is paid on the basis of income week by week, but liability is calculated annually, and an adjustment is made at the end of the year. This is the normal pattern of administration throughout the world; only Eire has followed Britain in adopting a system of cumulative payment. The main reasons for this general preference appear to be reduced administrative costs and greater flexibility. Non-cumulative payment requires an annual assessment of income for each taxpayer and may require an annual return of income from all taxpayers. This adds to administrative costs; however, this is offset by the fact that withholding of tax from income during the year can be undertaken on a much more rough and ready basis because errors can be corrected at the end of the year. The scale of the movements operation which keeps track of workers changing jobs can be greatly reduced. Securing accurate deductions of tax from subsidiary sources of income becomes much less important. Cumulative PAYE probably imposes slightly higher costs on employers, who have to keep track of a worker's earnings history; but because the amount of tax deducted from pay is usually correct, the number of cases where tax refunds are needed at the end of the tax year, or where under-payments have to be recouped subsequently, is considerably reduced. Cumulation under PAYE is much easier to operate if the rate structure includes a wide basic-rate band. The reason is that income from sources other than earnings, particularly investment income, can readily be brought within the system only if most taxpayers will be taxed at the same rate. The absence of an end-year assessment also restricts the range of factors which can be taken into account in determining liability. It is unlikely that British administrative procedures could readily be used to operate either the elaborately graduated rate structure or the wide range of deductions allowable from income which characterise the American income tax system. The argument can be used in either direction. Many people might not regard restrictions on the degree of complexity which can be incorporated in the UK income tax system as unwelcome, but others might be upset that it excluded — for example — a local income tax.

Similar choices exist within the benefit system. For many benefits at present, the period of assessment is fairly lengthy — six months or a year — but the level of benefit paid for that time is based on income over a much shorter period, commonly five weeks. If annual income tax liability was based on income during one particular month of the year, the system would be the subject of abuse and of protest. The disincentive to work in the chosen month would be enormous, while in the rest of the year it would be greatly reduced. To the extent that it was possible to respond to the opportunities afforded by such a system, revenue would be lost and the outcome would be evidently inequitable; to the extent that it was not, the result would be equivalent to using annual income, as at present. We can see no logic in this separation of period of assessment and period of payment, and no merit other than administrative convenience. Since we do not find it particularly convenient administratively, we do not consider it further as a serious possibility.

The major choices which confront us in the benefit system are those which need to be faced in the tax system also. Should entitlement or payment be cumulative or non-cumulative? If I am unemployed this week, should I get the same amount of benefit regardless of whether I was unemployed last week, or in a low-paid job, or a captain of industry. Once again, we are free to make separate decisions about liability and payment. It is possible to envisage that anyone who has a low income this week could be paid a certain amount in benefit, although his entitlement would be based on his earnings during the whole of the fiscal year. This means that anyone who had substantial earnings during some other part of the year would be receiving too much, and the excess would be recovered from his earnings at that time, or subsequently.

We regard cumulative tax liability, and non-cumulative benefit payment, as essential. If tax liability is non-cumulative, people with fluctuating incomes are liable to be treated in arbitrary and unfair ways (although a wide basic-rate band mitigates this). Benefit payments must be non-cumulative because many recipients are put in a position where they need money now, and it is impossible to suggest that they wait until the end of the year to see whether they are entitled to receive it.

This leaves two issues open. Should tax payments be cumulative or non-cumulative? Should benefit liabilities be cumulative or non-cumulative? As far as tax payments are concerned, we have little doubt that the wrong choice was made when cumulative PAYE was adopted in 1942; and that if the options we now have are those of going on as we are now, or of moving to a cruder, non-cumulative withholding system with end-year assessments and adjustments, we should begin to plan the change. However, when cumulative PAYE was adopted, no one imagined that it was possible for individuals to have magnetic cards which could record the allowances to which they were entitled, and had received; and which would each week initiate tax deductions and update themselves. If they had, it is possible that they might have favoured cumulative PAYE, and chosen to run it in a very different way. For these reasons, we think the choice between cumulation and non-cumulation in PAYE is now a finely balanced one.

Making benefit liability cumulative would imply that benefit entitlement would be based on annual, rather than current, income. This has significant advantages; weekly income often fluctuates, and does not reflect the underlying resources of the family, so that a longer-term basis for assessment would make the redistribution of the system more effectively targeted. We noted in Chapter 2 that one of the weaknesses of FIS is that it is assessed on the basis of income over a five-week period, but continues to be paid for a year. The result is that many of those receiving FIS in any one week are earning considerably more than a level which would entitle them to receipt. Similar observations apply to rent and rate rebates.

There is, however, a major disadvantage to cumulative benefit liability. If you receive benefit for part of the year, and have a higher income for the remainder of the year, you will have received more benefit than you should have obtained on an annual basis of assessment. It follows that someone who goes back to work after being unemployed is worse off in that job than someone who has the same earnings but has been in employment all the time. There is a persuasive logic to this. In effect, the unemployment benefit paid to a relatively well-off individual is treated as a loan which he will have to repay when his income rises. The difficulty is that this will be seen by him as a 'fine', which creates a significant disincentive ever to go back to work. It is true that he can only avoid the 'fine' by never going back to work, but the problem is no less real. A similar issue arises, although in less acute form, for low-paid or seasonal workers, whose incentive to find better-remunerated employment is correspondingly reduced. We are thus faced with the alternatives of giving benefits to individuals who do not really need them on the basis of a longer-run assessment of their requirements, or of imposing a − possibly substantial − financial penalty on those who succeed in improving their situation. The issue is familiar from the discussion of the merits of student grants and loans.

We consider that the arguments over the period of assessment for benefit are finely balanced. On the one hand, the choice of a long period enables us to relate benefits more effectively to need, on the other, there are efficiency costs. The choice is a decision which we leave open; our proposed administrative framework could be adapted to deal with either cumulative or non-cumulative assessment.

Appendix B: The tax and benefit unit

Few issues pose as many intractable problems for both tax and benefit systems as the choice of the unit on which income calculations are to be based. Most benefits are assessed on the basis of household income. Income tax is the liability of individuals, but the application of this principle is transformed by the provision that the income of married women is treated as if it were their husband's. In general in this book we have attempted to take the existing system as our starting point, but here we are shooting at a moving target. No one thinks the principles on which income tax are assessed are appropriate to the twenty-first century, or indeed the twentieth, and the case for some reform is universally acknowledged.[2]

There is, however, less agreement on what the direction of change should be. There is wide support for an individual basis for income tax; such wide support, in fact, that many of those who favour husband and wife being adopted as the tax unit, and would wish them to be able to transfer allowances to each other, wrongly describe their proposals as an individual basis for taxation. On the other hand, relatively few people would support an individual basis for benefits: this would imply that a dependent wife would have the same entitlement to benefit as a single person without resources, regardless of the income of her husband.

It is not essential to bring the two bases together, because the use of a common administrative procedure does not necessarily carry implications for the way in which either tax or benefits are calculated. This is clearly illustrated by the presence in the tax system of two distinct options. Under separate taxation, two spouses continue to make a joint return of income but their incomes are treated for tax purposes as if they were two separate individuals. Under separate assessment, they file separate returns.

There is, therefore, nothing in what we propose that would, of itself, require changes to the existing tax and benefit rules: each tax and benefit could continue on the variety of different procedures currently applied. Although greater homogeneity would be desirable, we think it inevitable, even in the long run, that the tax system will be closer to an individual basis than the benefit system. In giving benefits, we want to take account of the savings in housing, fuel, and other costs which people derive from living in units rather than separately, but it is unlikely that it will ever be acceptable to introduce into the tax system the penalty on marriage which consideration of the same issues would invite. We would also want to take account of the extent of actual or implied support of one partner for another, in a way that seems less appropriate for tax purposes. Benefit entitlement is properly that of the family as a whole; but liability for any withdrawal should be related to the income of individuals. So we suggest the splitting of withdrawal liability in proportion to the income of the spouses. In the case of a single-earner couple, this would mean that the breadwinner would be both legally and *de facto* subject to withdrawal. In the case of a two-earner couple, both benefit credit receipt and liability to withdrawal would be split in ratio of earnings. In fact, payment and withdrawal would be based on the previous year's earnings, with a small adjustment at end-year.

It is worth looking at a concrete example of how this would work. In Table 4.5 we look at the experience of a couple with a very complicated income pattern. We have deliberately chosen an example with significant fluctuations to show how the system would cope. In practice, only a small proportion of those in receipt of benefit credit would have earnings histories anything like as complicated as this. For ease of exposition, we treat the year as consisting of four weeks.

The couple we have chosen has two children, and rent of £17 and rates of £6 per week. The couple is therefore entitled to £72.25 per week in benefit credit under our base system, and this is the amount it would receive if it had no other income. In fact, both the partners here work, although the wife's part-time job is coming to an end. Last 'year' (four weeks!) the husband earned £350 while the wife earned £180. So this year we make the husband responsible for 66 per cent of the couple's benefit credit, or £47.70, while the wife is responsible for £24.55.

In the first week, the husband earned £100 and the wife £50. Both amounts were sufficient to remove entitlement to benefit credit, so net income is merely depressed by a tax payment. In week 2, this was true of the husband's income, while the wife had a small net receipt on her earnings of £40. In week 3, the husband's income fell to £50, so he received net benefit credit of £22.70 and paid no tax. In week 4, he again earned enough to extinguish his benefit credit entitlement, while the wife became entitled to £14.55 and paid no tax.

At the end of the year, annual tax liability and benefit entitlement would be calculated. This would show that this couple, because of its fluctuating income pattern, would have overpaid income tax by £6.73, but would have received more in benefit than its entitlement on an annual basis and would therefore have a net liability, which would be extinguished by increasing the band over which withdrawal applies. The two partners would be liable for this withdrawal in proportion to their earnings in the current year, this time in the ratio 74:26.

So we recommend the adoption of the family as the basis for benefit assessment, while income tax liability is individual. The family would receive the benefit credit, and the two spouses be jointly liable for withdrawal.

It is difficult to decide which member of the family unit should receive the benefit. One of the great advantages of child benefit, it is often argued, is that it is paid to the mother (and therefore available for expenditure on children). It would be possible to pay part of the benefit credit by post to a non-working mother, but to withdraw it again from the husband. This has considerable disadvantages. The

TABLE 4.5
Two-earner couple*: example of integrated system

A rules

Benefit credit

£18.00
+£30.35 for first child
+£ 5.50 for second child
+£18.40 80% of rent (£17) and rates (£6)

£72.25

Income tax credit: £16.13 husband, £10.30 wife
Income tax rate 30%
Withdrawal rate 50%

B payments

	Week 1	Week 2	Week 3	Week 4 £	'Annual'	'Last year'
(i) Earnings						
Husband	100	150	50	100	400 (74%)	350 (66%)
Wife	50	40	30	20	140 (26%)	180 (34%)

(ii) Tax and benefit payments (−) or receipts (+)

Husband					
Benefit credit	47.70	47.70	47.70	47.70	190.80
Income tax (net of tax credit)	−13.87	−28.87	0	−13.87	−56.61
Withdrawal	−47.70	−47.70	−25.00	−47.70	−168.10
net income	86.13	121.13	72.70	86.13	366.09

Wife					
Benefit credit	24.55	24.55	24.55	24.55	98.20
Income tax (net of tax credit)	−4.70	−1.70	0	0	−6.40
Withdrawal	−24.55	−20.00	−15.00	−10.00	−69.55
net income	45.30	42.85	39.55	34.55	162.25

(iii) Overall					
net income	131.43	163.98	112.25	120.68	528.34

C End-year calculation

Income tax liability = (£540 × 0.30) − (£16.13 × 4) − (£10.30 × 4) = £56.28.
The couple has paid £63.01, so they are due a refund of £6.73 (because the wife earned less at end of year).

On an 'annual' basis, benefit entitlement is (£72.25 × 4) − (£540.00 × 0.5) = £19. In fact the couple has received (£190.80 − £168.10) + (£98.20 − £69.55) = £51.35. There has been overpayment of benefit (net of tax) of £25.62. In consequence, next year's withdrawal band will be extended by £51.24, or £12.81 per week, divided between the partners in the ratio 74:26.

*Two children, rent £17, rates £6.

forced redistribution of considerable amounts of money from husband to wife might be resented by many people, including the authors of this book, who consider that the distribution of income between husband and wife is a matter for them rather than the Government. It would add to the administrative cost of the scheme, and would mean that all families would receive benefit and then all breadwinners would face a higher tax bill, whereas if benefit credit is calculated as part of the breadwinner's tax calculation no net item will be payable for the vast majority of people. We therefore believe that the best method of paying child benefit credit is through the pay-packet. Flat-rate child benefit could continue to be paid to the mother, unless the couple opted otherwise.

Our choice of the family as the unit for benefit purposes, which we consider essential, brings with it the problem, shared with the present system, of knowing what constitutes a family. It is difficult to think of any argument for providing more benefit to a cohabiting couple than we would give to the same two individuals if they were married. The present system (for supplementary benefit) asks people whether they are 'living together as man and wife', but the provisions are not enforced very rigorously; nor would we wish them to be. In the new system, the return filed by each person would ask if they were either receiving financial support from another person or whether living expenses were shared. If the answer to this was 'yes', then similar procedures to those for married couples would be adopted, if 'no', then they would be treated as single people.

References and notes

1. *Report of the Committee on the Enforcement Powers of the Revenue Departments*, Cmnd. 8822, London, HMSO (March 1983).
2. For a discussion, see J.A. Kay and C. Sandler, 'The Taxation of Husband and Wife: A View of the Debate in the Green Paper', *Fiscal Studies,* 3/3 (November 1982).

5

Distributional Changes

Basic principles

We have described in some detail in Chapter 1 how, and why, the
Beveridge scheme has failed. The extent of this failure is not in dispute.
The only source of support for the existing system is to be found in the
defensive reactions of a handful of DHSS officials. The Beveridge design
cost more than we have been willing to pay, and proved to be too in-
flexible to deal with the variety of sources of need.

Most of the serious criticism of current social security provision con-
centrates on one, or both, of two themes. One is the need for general
increases in the level of the main contingent benefits. Pensions and
child benefit are particularly favoured. The other is that there should
be an extension of the range of contingencies for which benefits are
provided. New benefits should be introduced, or the conditions of
eligibility for existing ones relaxed. These arguments have enjoyed a
certain amount of success. Pensions have risen relative to both earnings
and prices, although they remain a very low proportion of the average
earnings of the working population. The decline in the value of child
support has been arrested. The number of benefits has increased.
Single-parent families have been the subject of a bewildering variety of
new measures. Improvements have also been made to provision for the
disabled, although the level and coverage of these latter benefits remains
appallingly low.

The extent of progress in these directions is small, and for a straightforward reason. All these proposals demand additional expenditure
which governments of either political party have persistently been
reluctant to provide. It is, of course, possible to go on deploring this
fact indefinitely. The way in which the many pressure groups which
work for the different clients of the social security system continue,
year by year, to say essentially the same thing, is striking; and to some
extent it is right and proper that they should. But how much practical
help do potential beneficiaries obtain from this perpetual striving after
ideals which are probably unattainable, and certainly unattained? There

is certainly a case for considering how to do the best we can with the resources which we have. That is the subject of this chapter.

Our concern is with increasing the efficiency of the social security system. The scope for doing this is very large. We show how it is possible to reduce the basic rate of income tax by seven or eight points while systematically protecting the living standards of the worst off in society. Alternatively, we can virtually eliminate poverty, and give substantial additional benefit to low-income pensioners, within the existing social security budget. Or — and this is our central case — we can use the available savings partly to reduce taxes and partly to reduce poverty. This cuts the basic rate of income tax by 5 per cent while reducing by one-third the number of people with resources below 120 per cent of the existing supplementary benefit (SB) level. The choice between these possibilities is a matter of values rather than of analysis, but the potential of a more efficient system should interest all but some ludicrously doctrinaire figures who regard public expenditure as either desirable or undesirable for its own sake, regardless of what is done with it. The magnitude of the figures involved may be seen as a measure of the price which all of us, but most of all the poorest, are currently paying for the shibboleths of social insurance.

We discussed on pages 71–7 of Chapter 3 the basic principles involved in the design of an efficient social security system. We showed there that the twin objectives of relieving poverty while reducing the need for high marginal tax rates required that benefits should be both contingent and income related. To rely on contingent information alone implied considerable expenditure on benefits for households well above the poverty line, with consequently high tax rates on the population as a whole. To rely on income information alone, as with a single negative income tax applied to all kinds of household, requires unnecessarily high marginal rates of tax or very low assured levels of benefit provision.

The major part of the existing social security budget is devoted to purely contingent benefits, of which the most important are old-age pensions and child benefit. In Table 2.4, we demonstrated that almost half of all expenditure on old-age pensions, and over three-quarters of all expenditure on child benefit, goes to people who do not need what they receive, in the sense that they would not be poor even if they did not receive it. These benefits are not 'wasted'. They are intended to raise the standard of living of those who obtain them, and they do. But they are not required to achieve the principal objectives of our social security system. Their existence exerts constant downward pressure on the level of benefits paid to the poorest, because they raise the cost of any increase in these benefit levels. They also greatly increase the size of the overall social security budget and create the merry-go-round in which the state takes with one hand and gives back with another.

We therefore consider in this chapter the possible effects of a system that would channel the very considerable resources currently devoted to the support of children and the elderly more directly, and more exclusively, to those that need them. Under our present tax and social security arrangements there is no method of doing this that would not involve an additional enquiry into the means and resources of millions of households – an enquiry that would raise the costs of operating the system, would be resented by its victims, and would add to, rather than subtract from, the complexity of the system. Under the proposals we have put forward in Chapter 4, such measures are relatively easy to implement by suitable modifications to the structure of the PAYE system. They require no extra administration, no additional means tests, and little additional complication. The mechanism for achieving this system involves transforming what are currently purely contingent benefits into benefit credits.

We do not confine our attention to benefits alone. There are a number of tax allowances which principally serve social purposes. Their object is to help meet the differing needs of differing types of household. Most prominent among them are the married man's allowance and the age allowance. Age allowance is already cast as a nascent benefit credit. It is withdrawn, by reference to income, from relatively wealthy pensioners according to a formula which phases it out as income rises above £7,600 per annum. Although the married man's allowance is clearly indefensible in its present form, the most obvious and the most convincing rationale for it is as a contribution to the maintenance of a dependent spouse. We therefore explore the possibility of extending the precedent of age allowance and confining both these social tax allowances to relatively needy families.

The resources released by these modifications to the tax and benefit systems are potentially very large – around £10 billion at current tax and benefit levels. We consider the possibility of using them to reduce rates of tax, or to help poor households by means of a – now relatively cheap – across-the-board increase in benefit credits, or by making a more limited move in both of these directions.

There are arguments for contingent benefits which do not rest on their effectiveness in reducing poverty. But we should be clear from the outset of the terms of the debate. The issue is not whether we should help the old, or provide support for children. Under a benefit credit system, low-income families would continue to receive credits for old age or children. But credits for these contingencies would not be paid to high-income families. The question to be asked is, to what extent do we wish to transfer resources from households with above-average incomes and whose members are of working age, or childless, to other households with above-average incomes and whose members are elderly, or have children, simply because they are elderly or have children?

At present, we give the Dukes of Westminster child benefit for their families and retirement pensions when they grow old. We may do so for the practical reason that it is too difficult, or costly, or unpleasant to take these benefits away from some while continuing to give to others. But these practical problems can be overcome, and we have suggested ways in which, through a benefit credit scheme, they might be overcome. The issue which remains is whether there are reasons of more fundamental principle for continuing to pay these benefits even if we have an administrative system in which we are free to choose not to do so.

There seem to be four main groups of arguments in support of the status quo. One is based on the contributory principle: the Dukes of Westminster pay for their pensions and other benefits through national insurance contributions like anyone else. A second disputes the principle of means testing — it suggests that it is too difficult, or invidious, to distinguish between the Duke of Westminster and the rest of the population. Another view is that we should be concerned to redistribute income over the life cycle: the Duke of Westminster will need to spend more when his family is growing, and may see his income fall when he grows old, and he would value some assistance in planning for these contingencies. Finally, we may be concerned by some concept of horizontal equity or taxable capacity. Elderly dukes, or dukes with children, are worse off, or less able to make a contribution to national revenue, than similarly affluent dukes who are younger or who do not have family responsibilities.

It may be objected that we are deliberately ridiculing these arguments by illustrating them by application to one of the richest families in the country. On the contrary, we believe some *reductio ad absurdum* of this kind is essential to a clear perception of the issues involved. We are all sympathetic to the general cause of provision for the elderly, or for families with children, because we perceive, correctly, that the elderly and families, as a class, have greater needs than the rest of the population. We need to distinguish carefully between this argument and those which suggest that we should redistribute to elderly people and families who do not have greater needs than the population in general. To do this it is important to focus on households to which the payment of benefit clearly cannot be justified by reference to need.

Many old people may feel that they have somehow paid for their pensions. We examined in some detail in Chapter 1 the somewhat elusive concept of the contributory principle, and found it vacuous. But many old people can legitimately claim that they have been told that they have paid for their pensions, and the fact that the statement was untrue will not, and should not, moderate their sense of grievance at the prospect of losing them. A disturbing feature of attempts to pretend that national insurance contributions are something other than a tax is that it encourages people to think that they are themselves making provision for the future pensions which politicians have promised their children will pay. More importantly, plans have been made on the basis of an expectation of certain pension benefits and, whether or not these promises should have been made, it is now unreasonable to deviate too far from these expectations. This is not, of course, an argument against change; it is an argument against change which is sudden and without adequate transitional provisions.

A second group of arguments in favour of purely contingent benefits rests on the unpopularity of means tests. Much of this opposition is purely instinctive; to label a procedure a means test is to say one is opposed to it, and often to say little else. For this reason, we have tried to avoid the term as far as possible. It is clear that rational objection is not to means tests as such. The battle over whether the state could properly enquire into the resources of its citizens is one which was fought, vigorously, in the early nineteenth century when income tax was introduced, and re-echoed at the beginning of the twentieth century when the tax became progressive. No one now disputes that this kind of investigation is both proper and necessary. What is offensive are specific and potentially humiliating enquiries into the affairs of poor households which discriminate between them and the population as a whole. The intention of the proposals of Chapter 4 is to effect a considerable reduction in these enquiries by utilising much more extensively information which is, or could be, collected through the tax system. We expect that much of the opposition to the measures we suggest will be based on the assertion that they involve an extension of means testing. The assertion is about form rather than about substance; and to poor households the cost, in financial hardship and procedural unpleasantness, of this superficial sloganising is extremely high.

The expenditure requirements of an individual or a household rarely match their resources at every point during the life cycle. Typically, households will have greater needs, relative to their incomes, when there are young children in the family, and when they grow old and their income from work falls or disappears. Households will therefore need to reallocate their income over the life cycle, and may look to the state for help in this. It is necessary that this should be given to low-income households, whose capacity to save is limited, as is their access to credit markets. It is less obvious why the state should make similar provision for higher-income households, whose members can make these choices and arrangements for themselves. If someone who has enjoyed a high standard of living throughout his working career decides, through choice or imprudence, to make no provision for retirement income, does the state then have greater obligations to make provision for him than it does for citizens who have never enjoyed incomes at these levels?

Do pensioners, or households with children, have greater needs than the rest of the population? The two cases are clearly very different. The argument for pensions is that the elderly have similar needs but fewer resources; the argument for child support is that families with children have similar resources but greater needs. The needs of elderly people are not, in general, substantially greater than the needs of younger people at similar income levels, and there seems no justification on these grounds for providing pensions to well-off old people simply because they are old.

On the other hand, families at all income levels need to spend more to achieve the same standard of living as single people or couples without children. We should hesitate to say that they are actually worse off — after all, most couples with children are in this position as the result of a conscious choice — but their greater material needs might be considered a reason for providing state benefits or for demanding a smaller contribution to tax revenue.

This discussion has considered various possible objectives for a social security system, other than the relief of poverty. These objectives are not entirely without merit. There are reasons why the state should help people to plan their resources over their lifetime or why it should have regard to the needs even of relatively affluent families with children. But it is not enough that these ends are worthy ones; the issue is whether they have high priority among claims to the limited amount available for public expenditure on social security, or indeed in other areas. The question is not simply whether it is desirable to pay child benefit to wealthy households. It is whether it is more desirable to do this than to pay more child benefit to poor households. In what follows, we examine the consequences of a systematic abandonment of purely contingent benefits, in which pensions, child benefit, age allowance, and tax allowance for dependent spouses are strictly limited to those who need them.

In the remainder of this chapter, we first suggest some modifications of the most obvious peculiarities of the system we described in Chapter 4, rationalising the structure of child support and housing costs so as to put these benefits on a common basis for those in and out of work. In subsequent sections, we consider a sequential series of major changes to the base system. We begin by converting pensions and child benefit into benefit credits, thereby using the tax system to withdraw them from higher-income households. Next we transform the 'social' tax allowances – the married man's allowance and age allowance – into benefit credits. We then assess various alternative means of using the money saved by the implementation of these changes, and examine the overall consequences.

Integrating tax and national insurance contributions

National insurance contributions are already collected by the Inland Revenue through the PAYE system. However, the combination of these two taxes creates a very complex structure of marginal rates, as illustrated in Figure 5.1. Those below the national insurance floor pay no contributions or tax, but those immediately above face a tax bill of 9 per cent of all their income – or a marginal rate of many hundred per cent! Above the tax allowance, individuals who are not contracted out of the State Earnings-Related Pension Scheme (SERPS) pay 39 per cent of additional income until the national insurance ceiling, when this marginal rate falls to 30 per cent before it climbs back to 40 per cent

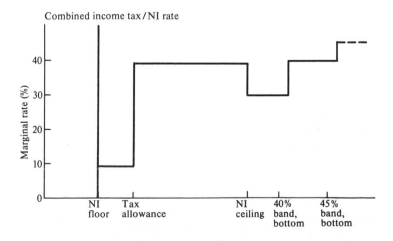

Fig. 5.1 Marginal rates in the existing system

and over as they enter the higher rates of income tax. The size of this 'hole' is greater for a married man than for a single person. We do not imagine anyone would wish to invent such a structure and have yet to hear any serious argument deployed in its favour.

Figure 5.2 shows a 'minimum change' option which would iron out some of the more obvious peculiarities. Under it, there is a basic rate of tax of 39 per cent. This starts from a level somewhat below the existing tax threshold. The reason is that an individual at the tax threshold currently pays 9 per cent of his whole income in national insurance contributions. The new basic-rate band extends to the point at which tax currently rises to 45 per cent; the existing 40 per cent band would be abolished. This scheme would create modest losses for someone

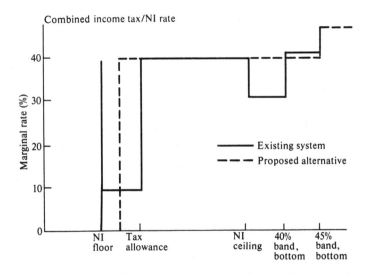

Fig. 5.2 The integration of income tax and national insurance

whose income is significantly above the upper earnings limit for national insurance contributions but below the point at which liability to the present 40 per cent rate begins. Some low-income working households are better off. We assume that other tax allowances – such as those for mortgage interest and pension contributions – continue to be given at 30 per cent rather than at the increased basic rate.

This would be facilitated if there were a separately earmarked social security tax. We noted in Chapter 1 that some of the arguments for the 'contributory principle' appear to be arguments for this kind of hypothecation, and we saw some merit in them. A possible approach is to impose a 9 per cent social security tax on taxable income. The base of the tax would be identical to that of income tax, with the (optional) exception that no allowance would be made for mortgage interest and pension contributions. The 40 per cent income tax rate band would be abolished, and the 45 per cent and higher-rate bands would be reduced by 9 per cent; thus the maximum rate of income tax would remain 60 per cent, comprising income tax at 51 per cent and social security tax at 9 per cent.

National insurance contributions are also a tax on employers, and it would simplify administration for both sides if they were transformed into a general payroll tax, which might be assigned to social security expenditure. So long as SERPS remains, which we hope will not be long, a subsidy equal to current contracting-out rates could be paid directly to occupational pension schemes. The legislation implementing this would facilitate adjustment to employee contribution rates, and for non-contributory contracted-out schemes those arrangements (if any) which were made when contracted-out contribution rates were reduced in 1978, would be unwound.

If we move to an earmarked social security tax, it is desirable that it should bear some relationship to social security expenditure. This would contrast with the present means of calculating national insurance contributions, where the link from expenditure to contribution rate is not only complicated, but has changed at least annually since 1976 as a result of the introduction, increase, and reduction of national insurance surcharges and of changes in the rate of Exchequer subsidy to the National Insurance Fund. Indeed, the apparently inveterate propensity of governments to interfere with these arrangements may give some cause for doubt as to how well a hypothecated tax would work in practice.

Once it is recognised that national insurance contributions are a tax, and not a payment related to prospective benefits, the rationale for restricting them to income from employment vanishes. We propose that the social security tax should apply to all income, including income from investments, pensions, and self-employment. The investment income surcharge would disappear, as would the present tax on the self-employed through Class 2 and Class 4 national insurance contributions. Pensions, and sickness and unemployment benefit, provided through a benefit credit mechanism, would be paid on the same basis to all those whose incomes were interrupted, regardless of the source of earnings prior to the interruption. The 'integrated base' presented at various stages in the chapter supposes tax and national insurance contributions brought together as described here, but no other changes in the structure of benefits or benefit credits.

Rationalising credits and rates

Because the taper on family income supplement (FIS) is so large, the rate at which benefits are withdrawn from households with children is at present much greater than the rate at which they are withdrawn from couples without children. We see no compelling rationale for this, and propose that the standard withdrawal rate for all working households should be 50 per cent.

A striking feature of the structure of the current system, as reflected in our 'base', is the difference between the way child support is provided for working households and the benefits given to one-parent, unemployed, or other household types. The basic reason for this is the difference between the structure of FIS and that of supplementary benefit (SB). Entitlement to FIS can only arise at all if there is at least one child in the household. It follows that the arrival of the first child can mean, for a low-paid worker, a FIS entitlement of as much as £22 per week; but FIS is not at all generous for subsequent children. Supplementary benefit, by contrast, offers a flat payment per child based on the age of the child, but independent of whether that child is the first or the fifth in a household.

There is a complex balance of arguments here, and the fact that they have been resolved in different directions for different benefits is the result of accident rather than of design. The costs of feeding and clothing a child tend to rise with its age. However, the presence of any child in a household tends to reduce the earning capacity of the mother, and the arrival of a second child has a much smaller effect. The structure we have chosen to adopt is one which provides a basic benefit credit of £9 per week per child. This is the minimum SB child addition under the present system. It is much less than the credit currently given to the first child in a family under FIS, but much more than that provided to FIS households for the second child and subsequent children. Additionally, however, we provide a further £7.50 per week for the first child in a household, and a supplement of £7.50 per week for each child under five. With this benefit structure, we would consider the case for specific 'one-parent' supplements to child benefit to be weak, and would propose to abolish them. We would stress that our principal concern here is to establish a common basis of child support for all households, whether working or not. We are less concerned with what that common basis should be, which should be the subject of specific enquiry: our figures are only intended as suggestions as to how a balance might be achieved. Similar observations apply to housing benefit, where there are currently two sets of rules. Claimants of supplementary benefit are entitled to have the whole of their housing costs paid; for others there is a more complex income-related formula. In finding a common basis, we have started from the proposition that it is undesirable that the state should pay the whole of anyone's housing costs. For pensioners and one-parent families, therefore, we set the benefit credit at 80 per cent of housing costs, in line with the level given for working families in Chapter 4.

Converting unconditional benefits into benefit credits

This is the single most important element in our reform package. What are at present unconditional benefits become benefit credits, which are therefore withdrawn from the better off. As we have noted, retirement pensions and child benefit are by far the most important unconditional benefits in the present system. Child benefit is replaced by an additional benefit credit of £6.50 per week per child. The state pension is replaced by a pensioner credit of £36.90 per week for a couple and £21.50 for a single person, which with the individual benefit credits gives a total sum equal in value to the existing state pension. The total saving in public expenditure is approximately £5.5 billion at 1983/4 prices and post-November 1983 benefit rates. The position of poor households remains unaffected by these changes. Recipients of FIS, or pensioners without resources other than the state pension, would be no worse off than at present; indeed, because of the new automaticity of benefit payment, many of them would gain significantly from the increased likelihood of receiving benefit. All savings come from reductions in the benefits paid to higher-income households.

Although our treatment of pensions and child benefit means they make more or less equal contributions to the total reduction in public expenditure, the impact of the two changes is very different. Most current recipients of child benefit would lose entitlement; of the children for whom benefit is currently paid, 63 per cent would be in households which would receive no benefit credit whatever. In contrast, few pensioners have substantial income from other sources. Almost everyone of pension age would continue to receive some pension, and the greater part of overall pension expenditure would continue.

Converting tax allowances to benefit credits

While querying the role of benefits which are currently paid to all households, regardless of need, it is appropriate to look at those tax allowances which serve a similar purpose. It is not easy to determine the purpose of any particular tax allowance, since the tax system has in the main developed by historical accident rather than by design. However, it would seem that some tax allowances — such as those on mortgage interest or pension contributions — owe their existence to public anxiety to support particular *activities*, such as owner-occupation or retirement saving. Other allowances seem mainly intended to favour particular kinds of *household* — these include the married man's allowance and the age allowance for elderly taxpayers. Although the distinction cannot be a precise one, the underlying principle is clear. On the one hand, industrial building allowances exist because we wish to favour the construction of industrial buildings, and not because people who construct industrial buildings are thought to be particularly needy. On the other hand, the married man's allowance and the age allowance exist not primarily because the state wishes to encourage marriage or longevity, but because it perceives (or did at some time perceive) married men and elderly people as being more deserving than the rest of the population.

These latter allowances serve essentially the same function as state benefits — indeed, it is only since 1979 that state support for children has entirely taken the form of cash grants rather than income tax allowances. We therefore examine the possibility of also converting these allowances into benefit credits, so that enhanced allowances for elderly households or those with only one earner would be provided for low-income families, but not for the population at large. In fact, age allowance already has a 'taper' which removes its value from high-income groups. Thus it already has the form of a benefit credit, and we do no more than apply this principle more extensively and to other allowances.

The additional allowance given to a married man, as compared with a single individual, is worth £5.85 per week to the basic-rate taxpayer. We suggest that the allowance be abolished[1] and the first adult benefit credit increased by this amount. The value of the additional tax allowances given to pensioners is currently £3.30 per week for a single pensioner and £5.50 for a married couple. Conversion of these to benefit credits implies revenue losses as well as gains. The reason is that there are many pensioners whose incomes are too low for age allowance to be of value to them, but who would be recipients of a benefit credit.

The principal beneficiaries of age allowance are middle-income pensioners, and conversion of the allowance to a benefit credit spreads some of that benefit over lower-income pensioner households. Among working married couples, by contrast, the number whose incomes are too low for the married man's allowance to be of value is insignificant. The total saving from these measures is around £3 billion.

Using the money: increasing benefit credits and reducing the basic tax rate

The measures we have described in the preceding sections would, in aggregate, yield savings of over £10 billion at 1983/4 prices and tax and benefit rates. They are achieved while substantially protecting the position of poor households. They are the result of the systematic application of a single principle. State support should not be provided on a basis which is solely contingent on household type but independent of income level. While contingent benefits remain, they should be phased out as incomes increase.

There are many ways in which revenue gains of this magnitude could be used. We outline the effect of using them in two ways; roughly half is used to effect a reduction in the basic rate of income tax from 30 per cent to 25 per cent, while the remainder is used primarily to increase the incomes of poor households.

In Chapter 4 we replicated the effects of the existing tax and benefit systems through a tax credit and a benefit credit. For a single person, tax allowances were replaced by a tax credit of £10.30 per week and, in addition, a benefit credit of £12.50 per week was substituted for housing and other benefits. The equivalent figures for a married man were £16.13 and £18. The transformation of the married man's allowance into a benefit credit reduces the tax credit for a married man to that of a single person − £10.30 − but raises his benefit credit correspondingly. A couple would therefore receive a total benefit credit of £23.85 per week.

One objective of our proposals is to use some of the resources thus released to improve the position of poor working households. As an illustration of how this might be achieved, we increase the benefit credit for a single person from £12.50 to £20 per week and for a couple from £23.85 to £30 per week. We do this by instituting an adult benefit credit of £10 per week and a further credit of £10 per week for the first adult child in a household. A 'first adult' rule of some kind is a consequence of any reform, even cosmetic, of the overtly sexist married man's allowance, while the tax treatment of single people is constrained

TABLE 5.1
Restructuring the tax and benefit systems
(£ p.w., 1983/4 prices)

	Base system	After NI integration	Distributional changes (1) Rationalise credits and rates	(2) Housing
Working families				
Single credit	12.50	–	–	–
Couple credit	18.00	–	–	–
First child < 5	30.35	–	24.00	–
First child > 5	30.35	–	16.50	–
Subsequent children	5.50	–	9.00	–
Proportion of housing	0.80	–	–	–
Withdrawal				
With children	0.50	–	–	–
No children	0.25	–	0.50	–
Tax credit – husband	16.13	–	–	–
wife	10.30	–	–	–
Basic rate of income tax (%)	0.30	0.39	–	–
One-parent families				
Single credit	12.50	–	–	–
One-parent addition	7.00	–	–	–
Child 0–10	9.15	–	As working family	–
Child over 10	13.70	–		–
Proportion of housing	1.00	–	–	0.80
Withdrawal	0.50	–	–	–
Tax credit	16.13	–	–	–
Basic rate of income tax (%)	0.30	0.39	–	–
Pensioners				
Single credit	0.20	–	–	–
Couple credit	0.40	–	–	–
Single pension	34.05	–	–	–
Couple pension	54.50	–	–	–
Proportion of housing	1.00	–	–	0.80
Withdrawal	0.20	–	–	–
Tax credit – single	13.62	–	–	–
couple	21.67	–	–	–
Basic rate of income tax (%)	0.30	0.39	–	–

TABLE 5.1 continued

	Distributional changes		
(3) Convert unconditional to income-assessed	(4) Convert additional allowances to benefit credits	(5) Increase benefit credits	(6) Reduce basic tax rate
–	–	20.00	20.00
–	23.85	30.00	30.00
30.50	–	35.50	35.50
23.00	–	28.00	28.00
15.00	–	15.50	15.50
–	–	–	0.80
–	–	–	0.50
–	–	–	0.50
–	10.30	–	8.58
–	–	–	8.58
–	–	–	0.34
–	–	20.00	20.00
–	5.85	–	5.85
As working family	–	As working family	As working family
–	–	–	0.80
–	–	–	0.50
–	10.30	–	8.58
–	–	–	0.34
34.25	37.57	80.00	80.00
54.90	60.44	115.00	115.00
–	–	–	–
–	–	–	–
–	–	–	0.80
–	–	–	0.20
–	10.30	–	8.58
–	10.30	–	8.58
–	–	–	0.34

by the fact that the tax group brings together such disparate types of people as juveniles living at home, one-parent families, and widows. The household principle provides a basis for discrimination. Couples with children would receive an additional £5 per week on the first-child credit. In our judgement this measure, together with the explicit recognition of the responsibility for household support as an element of the benefit system, makes further special provision for single parents unnecessary.

We have maintained a special pensioner credit, and envisage that some contingent benefit should continue for pensioners and the sick and unemployed, although it should be a benefit credit rather than an unconditional benefit. The form which these credits should take requires some consideration. Their rationale is that they are a substitute for earnings when earnings capacity is restricted, and this suggests that they should be paid on the same basis as earnings; taxed, and treated as income in the withdrawal of other benefit credits. At the same time, as benefit credits they would be withdrawn by other income. Although this sounds rather cumbersome, it has the major advantage that it allows a direct relationship to be established between earnings, and benefits paid in lieu of earnings. It is because there is no such direct relationship at present that concern has grown up about replacement rates for those who retire or lose their jobs. Within the revenue constraints we have imposed, a pensioner credit of this kind could be set at £85 per week for a couple and £60 for a single person. Because pensioners would receive fewer tax allowances than at present, this figure is not directly comparable with the current pension rates of £34.05 and £54.50 per week; but it is nearly so, and for a representative pensioner with no resources other than the state pension the increase in net spending power would be of the order of 25 per cent.

The changes summarised

Table 5.1 summarises the changes outlined above. It shows the structure of benefit and tax credits as they would affect working families, one-parent families, and pensioners, and shows how these change as the various steps of reform are accomplished. The first two columns show our 'base' system from Chapter 4, before and after the integration of income tax and national insurance contributions. The next two columns consist of the rationalisation of credits and rates, and the extension of a uniform level of housing support. Steps (3) and (4) are the main revenue-raisers, with child benefit and the pension taken from richer units, and the abolition of the married man's allowance and the age

Table 5.2
Revenue forgone/gained under various stages of reform
(£m., 1983/4 prices)

Cumulative change from existing system with:	Revenue forgone (−) or gained (+)
New basic system	+60
Rationalise child support etc.	+1,060
Housing to 80%	+1,550
Pension and child benefit to benefit credits	+7,020
With married man's allowance and age allowance	+10,270
Increase benefit credits	+5,820
Final system (with basic tax rate cut)	+600

allowance. Step (5) spends money on the poor, while step (6) reduces the basic rate of income tax.

Table 5.2 summarises the estimated revenue effects of the different stages of reform. The rationalisation of child support etc. raises about £1 billion, the reduced percentage for housing some £500 million, and the conversion of unconditional benefits to benefit credits £5.5 billion, with an additional £3.2 billion from the abolition of tax allowances. The available £10.2 billion is then spent almost equally on increasing benefit credits and reducing the basic rate of income tax.

Overall, there is a net revenue gain of around £600 million. We would propose that a substantial proportion of that revenue should be used to increase some of the minor social security benefits, particularly those for the disabled and those helping them. It would be agreed by almost all that many of these benefits, which go to those who have suffered misfortunes through no possible fault of their own, are outrageously low; but in the context of acute overall pressure on the total social security budget, action to increase them has never attracted political priority.

Consequences

The changes we have described in this chapter are wide ranging. Although each can be defended on individual merits, the overall consequences are not obvious. In this section, we analyse these consequences by reference to several criteria. How do they affect the distribution of income between different types of household? How do they affect people at different income levels within any broad category of household? After examining distributional effects in these two different ways, we look at the incentive effects of the changes by examining their impact on marginal rates of tax — the proportion of any additional earnings which is lost as a result either of tax or of the withdrawal of benefit. We then consider the effect on the numbers in poverty, and also on 'replacement rates'.

I: Redistribution between household types

Table 5.3 shows how the average income of different types of household is affected by the measures described in the preceding sections. The detailed changes which each stage implies to the structure of the system are given in the final appendix. The overall average net income after tax and benefits is more or less unchanged, confirming that our proposals could, assuming that behaviour is unchanged, be revenue-neutral. Pensioners and large families with a single source of income are

TABLE 5.3
Average net incomes under various stages of reform
(£ p.w., 1983/4 prices)

Type of family	Existing system (post-Nov. 1983 benefits, 1983/4 tax)	New basic system	With: (1) Rationalise Child support and tax rates	(2) Housing to 80%	(3) Pension and child benefit to benefit credits	(4) With married man's allowance and age allowance	(5) Increase benefit credits	(6) Final system (with basic tax rate cut)
Single	109.11	108.66	107.25				107.59	112.96
One-parent family	100.78	100.27	96.99	94.31	88.33	90.78	96.47	98.38
Couple (WNW)	145.55	143.66	142.21			136.42	136.61	143.84
+1	155.91	154.55	153.90		147.80	142.51	144.83	151.97
+2	161.77	160.89	160.10		149.69	145.60	149.92	157.00
+3	167.08	166.82	168.44		154.77	151.91	158.88	165.93
+4+	185.72	184.50	188.69		177.94	176.26	185.24	192.02
Couple (WW)	192.17	191.96	191.27			185.53	185.64	194.23
+1	187.62	188.18	187.90		181.57	175.49	176.33	184.38
+2	191.28	191.40	191.16		178.82	173.41	175.09	183.03
+3	212.30	211.85	211.16		194.62	190.34	194.02	202.40
+4+	181.53	182.61	184.91		167.82	165.78	173.87	180.52
Single pensioner	54.20	54.57	52.19	50.24	42.42	42.29	53.88	56.24
Couple pensioner	91.58	92.78	89.69	88.14	73.26	69.57	89.70	93.04
Average, above groups	132.24	132.18	130.69	129.97	122.68	119.47	125.98	131.63

Notes: (i) WNW = wife not working. WW = wife working. (ii) Figures are not repeated above, they remain constant in a subsequent step.

among the groups to be net gainers. These are the intended beneficiaries of the measures we have suggested to help poor working families and the largest group of poor households – the elderly. The overall gain by pensioners as a class masks, as we shall see later, very substantial redistribution within this group, from better-off to worse-off pensioners.

It may seem surprising, and to many undesirable, that the largest gains are made by single people and two-earner couples without children. However, this is an inevitable result of *any* policy which reduces social benefits in order to reduce taxation. These groups obtain very little in benefit, and pay comparatively large amounts of tax.

II: Redistribution between income groups

Figure 5.3 shows the pattern of gains and losses within each category of household. The picture here is clear. In all groups, poor households gain and richer households lose. There could hardly be a clearer demonstration that neither redistribution nor an effective social security system require either high tax rates or high levels of public expenditure. The degree of redistribution is especially marked amongst pensioners. Although the extent of Government expenditure on pensioners is very large, the efficiency with which it is directed is very low. The measures put forward in this chapter almost completely eliminate poverty among the elderly at very little net revenue cost.

III: Marginal rate effects

Table 5.4 shows the distribution of marginal rates of tax before and after reform. These marginal tax rates include not only income tax but also national insurance contributions, social security tax, and the implicit rates which result from benefit withdrawal. For most non-pensioners, there is a reduction in the marginal tax rate they face. The most common experience is a fall from 39 per cent to 34 per cent as a consequence of the five-point cut in the basic rate of tax. 77 per cent of households now face a marginal tax rate of 34 per cent or less. However, there is a substantial minority who suffer increases in their marginal effective rate of tax, and the overall average of marginal tax rates rises. Those affected in this way are mainly the heads of large families. We have explained repeatedly how this is an inevitable consequence of measures to mitigate the poverty and unemployment traps. These necessarily involve an improvement in the relative position of those low-paid workers at the upper end of the poverty trap. This can only be achieved at feasible cost if the differential between these and the somewhat higher paid is narrowed.

We are conscious that although the proposals we have made reduce

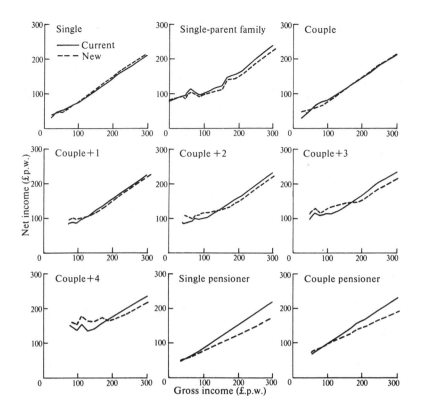

Fig. 5.3 Redistribution between income groups

the tax rates faced by the majority of the population, there is a substantial minority — around 15 per cent of the population — who would face very high effective marginal rates of tax on their extra earnings. For a significant number of people, the marginal tax rate would actually be increased.

The reason for this is that our proposals, while integrating tax payment and benefit receipt for administrative purposes, also reduce the overlap between tax and benefits which is a justly criticised feature of the present system. The group which faces high marginal tax rates consists, broadly speaking, of those who are net recipients of state support. The bulk of the population makes net contributions through the direct tax system and for this majority the burden of taxation is reduced, in terms of both average and marginal rates.

Do we need to 'institutionalise the poverty trap', as we expect our critics will observe? Can high marginal tax rates on the poor be avoided?

TABLE 5.4

Marginal rates under the new system before national insurance integration, and after 5 per cent basic rate tax cut and benefit increases

	> 100	80–100	60–80	40–60	< 40	Average
Before:						
Non-pensioner	–	6	4	5	85	40.7
Pensioner	–	–	–	24	76	30.9
After:						
Non-pensioner	–	19	–	24	77	44.1
Pensioner	–	–	–	100	–	54.0

We are forced, reluctantly, to conclude that they cannot. We have seen no practical scheme which avoids this difficulty, except by accepting a worse evil; a substantial reduction in the level of support for the poor, or high marginal tax rates on a much higher proportion of the population. Indeed, in order to eliminate tax rates in excess of 100 per cent, which we believe are ethically indefensible, we have had to accept some cost on these counts. Some sort of poverty trap is the price we unavoidably pay for guaranteeing households a minimum level of state support.

The best is frequently the enemy of the good, and realism is a disadvantage in advocacy. It can be argued that, because we have not fulfilled a set of logically incompatible objectives, we should not accept what is possible and wait for something to be devised which does meet these criteria. The wait may prove to be a lengthy one.

Marginal tax rates faced by pensioners are most increased. Clearly, work incentives are not so much at issue here, but savings incentives are. If private provision for retirement is heavily taxed, then the incentive to save during a working lifetime is correspondingly diminished. But there is a range of different factors here, working in conflicting directions. Higher-income groups will wish to save more, reflecting the reduction in the degree of state support they can expect in old age. Lower-income groups may save less, because the basic level of state retirement provision has been increased. The marginal tax rate of 100 per cent on the savings of pensioners dependent on supplementary benefit is eliminated. But many pensioners with incomes above this level will face an increased marginal tax rate on their savings. On balance, we think a move from income to expenditure taxation a much more effective and efficient stimulus to personal saving for retirement

TABLE 5.5

Numbers with incomes below 100 per cent and 120 per cent of
supplementary benefit under existing system, new base system
and after distributional reforms
(Number '000)

	Under existing system (1983/4)	Under existing system if full take-up and no discretion	Under new base system with integrated tax and NI	Under new system distributional reforms
(i) *Below supplementary benefit*				
Single (non-pensioner)	6	–	–	–
One-parent families	3	–	–	–
Couples (non-pensioner)	22	26	16	16
Couples with children	40	25	3	3
Single pensioners	800	20	–	64
Couple pensioners	385	–	–	–
All	1,256	71	19	83
(ii) *Below supplementary benefit + 20%*				
Single (non-pensioner)	6	–	–	–
One-parent families	3	–	–	–
Couples (non-pensioner)	34	52	32	63
Couples with children	61	43	9	6
Single pensioners	1,960	2,080	2,090	1,511
Couple pensioners	991	1,065	1,055	627
All	3,055	3,240	3,186	2,207

Notes: (i) Households are here regarded as facing an income deficiency if their total income after receipt of all benefits, but after deduction of housing costs, is less than 120 per cent of the SB scale rate applicable to their family size.

(ii) This table excludes the unemployed, for which the new system makes little difference.

than indiscriminate largesse to the elderly regardless of their means or opportunities.

IV: Effects on numbers in poverty

In Table 5.5 we examine the effects our distributional changes would have on the number of people with low incomes. The table presents

TABLE 5.6

Effect on numbers with income below 120 per cent of
supplementary benefit

(Numbers '000)

	Existing system (1983/4)	After reforms:	
		(i) with 5% base rate cut increases in benefit credits	(ii) with large rises in benefit credits for pensioners
Single (non-pensioner)	6	–	–
One-parent families	3	–	–
Couple (non-pensioner)	34	63	63
Couple with children	61	6	6
Single pensioners	1,960	1,511	293
Couple pensioners	991	627	41
All	3,055	2,207	403

estimates of the number with incomes, after deduction of housing costs, below the SB scale rates, and with incomes below 120 per cent of these rates. Some 1.3 million family units are estimated as 'poor' on the basis of their current receipts, largely because of non take-up of benefits. If all benefits were taken up to their full estimated entitlement, this figure would fall to below 100,000. Our new base system, with full take-up assumed because of the automaticity of benefit payment, would reduce this further.

The results of the distributional reforms have more impact on the incomes of those at or around the SB scale rate. The lower half of Table 5.5 shows how many people have incomes below this level under the various systems. At present in excess of 3 million do, and this is slightly increased by the assumed removal of discretionary benefit payments. The distributional reforms suggested would reduce the number of people with incomes below 120 per cent of the SB level by some 900,000 to 2.2 million.

If reducing poverty was the primary goal, this could be achieved even more effectively by spending the whole of the £10 billion on rises in the benefit credit, with the addition all going to pensioners. This would enable the incomes of the poorest single pensioners to rise by some £17 per week, and that of the poorest couple pensioners to rise by some £25 per week, compared to their present entitlements. Table 5.6 shows the dramatic effect this would have on the number with incomes below 120 per cent of the SB scale. The number is reduced from 3 million to only 400,000.

V: The relationship between incomes in and out of work

One of the most difficult questions to be answered in the field of social security is how best to preserve incentives to seek or retain work while at the same time protecting the living standards of those without a job. A large part of the reason for this dilemma is that the benefit system attempts to provide for needs – which may include sizeable payments to cover the expenses of children or housing – while wages, the prime source of income for those in work, are solely related to the characteristics of the individual. The result is that, for someone with a large number of children or high housing costs but with abnormally low wages, it is possible for income when unemployed to approach, or even to exceed, income in work.

Under the current system, the major benefits the unemployed and sick receive are the national insurance benefits. These are now given at a flat rate (earnings-related supplements were abolished at the beginning of 1982) and are taxable (as from July 1982). For those with no other income this is generally insufficient to bring their 'resources' above their 'needs' as measured by the SB scale rates, particularly if they have children or high housing costs, so many of the unemployed have also to claim supplementary benefit. With the introduction this year of housing benefit, those in privately rented accommodation will have to go to a third party for their housing assistance. After a year, entitlement to national insurance benefits ceases, and individuals become dependent on supplementary benefit.

It is now the case that the incomes of most of the sick or unemployed are determined by supplementary benefit and not by national insurance benefits. The long-term unemployed, and those with an incomplete contributions record but with housing costs or children, are partly dependent on it. The only major groups which receive the national insurance benefit alone are those with working spouses or other income.

We saw in Chapter 2 that the relationship between incomes in and out of work has in the past been a cause for serious concern. This was largely because the fact that benefits were not subject to tax could lead to large tax rebates for short periods of unemployment, and because of the existence of earnings-related supplements to unemployment benefit. Both of these problems were removed in 1982, and the number of people who are actually better off out of work is now very small. Further improvement in the relationship is now a much less pressing priority than it was in, say, 1978. Nevertheless, the problem continues to exercise a large number of commentators, as evidenced by the weight of submissions on this subject to the recent Treasury and Civil Service Committee inquiry.[2] So in what follows, we explore ways of improving the relationship further. We have two objectives in doing so; we wish to reduce high replacement rates while retaining or improving the position of the unemployed on average. We thus wish to lower the percentage with replacement rates over 90 per cent, but to increase the average replacement rate.

At a very simple level, there are two ways to increase the incentive to work rather than to be unemployed. Either you can reduce the incomes of the unemployed or you can increase the incomes of those in work. It is, we hope, unlikely that a political concensus for systematic adoption of the first course of action will emerge. The second can be achieved by the release of significant amounts of money to help the working poor.

There is a very strong argument for increasing the housing and child credits paid to the working poor to at least a level similar to that which they receive if unemployed. The major reason for high replacement rates is the generosity of the current system to the unemployed if they have many children or high housing costs; if these elements are at least symmetrical as between the working and the unemployed populations, then the problem is removed. In the present system, some attempt is made to do this by providing FIS, housing benefit, and child benefit to those in work in order to balance receipt of supplementary benefit when unemployed. Child benefit is a particularly powerful tool, for as it is counted as income for SB purposes it only benefits those in work.

However, the present system provides benefits for the working poor which are different from those given to the unemployed, and often considerably lower. In the reforms outlined in this chapter, we improve the position of the working poor considerably by increasing child credits with the money generated by the retrenchment of contingent benefits. Table 5.7 shows what happens to replacement rates if the unemployed are treated as in the present system but the reforms for the working poor are implemented.

There are three main effects. First, and most important, the number of people with replacement rates over 80 per cent is cut from 13 per cent of the working population under the present system to 9 per cent with the reforms; raising child credits for those in work is a very effective way of reducing high replacement rates — and is considerably more cost-effective than a child benefit rise. Those with higher incomes are affected in two different directions. The replacement of child benefit by child credits increases average replacement rates, while the basic-rate cut reduces them.

TABLE 5.7

The relationship between incomes in and out of work

Short-term average replacement rates (RR) (13-week spell of unemployment):

	Under existing system (1983/4 tax, post-November 1983 benefits)	With distributional reforms (Table 5.1, col. 6)
Percentage of working heads with		
RR below 0.5	31	35
0.5–0.8	56	56
0.8–1.0	11	8
over 1.0	2	1
Average RR	0.589	0.581

Long-term average replacement rates (52-week spell of unemployment):

Percentage of working heads with		
RR below 0.5	31	35
0.5–0.8	56	56
0.8–1.0	11	8
over 1.0	2	1
Average RR	0.583	0.581

Sources: IFS calculations from 1981 Family Expenditure Survey. The methodology followed is that of A.W. Dilnot and C.N. Morris, 'Modelling Replacement Rates', IFS Working Paper 39, London, Institute for Fiscal Studies (1982).

As we discussed in Chapter 4, the question of the period over which benefits should be assessed is particularly important for the unemployed. There are strong arguments in favour of making benefit assessment annual, so that payment is more effectively targeted on those who have long-term need. There is a strong case that unemployment benefit should not be paid to a company director who leaves one job and spends a month looking for his next. Considerations like this would lead to an annual basis for assessment, such as that proposed earlier for the working population. In this case, short-term receipt of benefits would be withdrawn from those with sufficient income in the rest of the year; for them, unemployment benefit would become a loan. This in turn means that their replacement rate as conventionally measured, for a short period of unemployment, would fall; unemployment would carry with it a much more severe financial penalty.

The acceptance of an annual basis of assessment for benefit receipt carries with it a penalty in that those returning to work after a relatively short period have to pay back the implied loan. In certain cases the repayment, as a proportion of net income, could be very large for a considerable period. An example may help to clarify the problem. Suppose an individual (single with no housing costs, for simplicity) works for ten weeks, earning £100 per week, and then becomes unemployed for ten weeks. Assuming a withdrawal rate of 50 per cent, in the first ten weeks he would have his benefit credit of £12.50 per week wholly withdrawn by half of his income. In the second ten weeks he would receive a benefit credit of, say, £30 per week while unemployed. If he then returns to work he becomes liable for the £300 he received while unemployed, which would in practice be withdrawn in the next year by extending the band of income over which withdrawal was made, so that instead of using £50 to extinguish his benefit credit while working, he would pay an additional £5.77 (£300/52) per week to 'repay' his receipt while unemployed. If he remained unemployed for more than a year, his liability for repayment during this year could not exceed the earnings which had not already been used for withdrawal — in this case, 50 per cent of £500 (ten weeks at £50).

The advantages, in terms of equity generated by a longer-term basis of assessment, and in terms of efficiency of creating a similar system of support for working and unemployed families with children and for housing costs, are thus balanced by an efficiency loss created by this fixed penalty for return to work. These conflicts, as we stressed in Chapter 3, are inevitable, and are the source of many of the difficulties which exist in the present system. The problem exists, though in a less severe form, for working families with fluctuating incomes; there, if an individual is offered more money after a period of low earnings, he faces the problem that he may then have to pay back his previous benefit credit receipt.

We consider that these arguments are finely balanced. On the one hand, the choice of a long period enables us to relate benefit more effectively to need. On the other, there are efficiency costs. The choice is a decision which we leave open; our proposed administrative framework, which we now develop, could be adapted to either cumulative or non-cumulative assessment.

Conclusions

The primary purpose of the proposals we have put forward in this chapter is to suggest a broad direction of change. They are the result of a single-minded pursuit of the principle that it is inappropriate for the state to provide purely contingent benefits, and that entitlement should be based on need, liberally interpreted and liberally administered. We have shown that as a means of dealing with what we see as the primary objective of a social security system – the relief of poverty – the principle is very effective. The reforms presented here achieve a great deal more than the present system, at considerably lower cost, and without the gross anomalies and complexities which characterise our present arrangements.

Some of the resistance to this redirection of our approach to social security will represent no more than the ritual incantation of familiar systems. Although we have shown at length that the concept of social insurance has long ceased to have much effect on what people actually do – in reality, it never had much effect on what people actually did – we have also observed that it continues to have an enormous effect on what people say. We expect that others will reject what we suggest because it involves an extension of means-tested benefits. Means-tested benefits are unpopular because the reputation of the means-tested benefits of the thirties will not easily die. Nor is it encouraged to die by the current 4 million who annually submit to detailed enquiry into their household circumstances in order to establish their entitlement to supplementary benefit or supplementary pension. This is a process which many people find offensive and demeaning. Under our proposals, the need for it would substantially disappear; only those with special needs or problems which the benefit credit system failed to meet would find their resources and their habits the subject of individual enquiry. The need for means tests largely disappears because the system makes effective use of the information which is already collected for everyone in order to administer income tax (and which will go on being needed in order to administer income tax whatever changes are made to the present system).

There are other arguments for contingent benefits which suggest that we should wish to support people in certain contingencies even if these contingencies do not cause them any hardship. Should individuals be helped to rearrange their resources over their lifetime? Most of us will have children at some time during our lives, and all of us one day hope to be old. We may look to the state for protection against hardship during these periods. If the managing director of ICI chose to make no provision for his retirement, then we would wish to offer the same protection against destitution that we offer to everyone else, but it is not clear to us why our obligations should extend any further. And if, as is more likely, he is provided with a company pension and cushioned by his own savings, we do not see why the payment of a pension to him simply on the grounds that he is old should command high priority in the allocation of public expenditure.

Should we be more ready to support the children of better-off tax-payers? It is true that a family with children will have a lower material standard of living at a given level of income than a childless couple, since it costs more to buy the same goods for three or more. But it hardly makes sense to say that the family is worse off, since the parents have chosen to have children and have done so for reasons of personal pleasure rather than social obligation. What, then, is the source of the claim on the rest of society, and why should it rank equal to the claim of children of low-income families to be given some protection from the poverty of their parents?

The case for contingent benefits seems strongest for unemployment benefit: unemployment is generally involuntary, and it is difficult to insure against unemployment in private markets. The idea of insurance began in this area, and it is the one in which it retains a measure of validity. We acknowledge that the objectives of a social security system are complex. But we have also demonstrated the failure of the existing system to achieve its present objectives at a politically acceptable cost. Given this, we believe that the case for concentration on these principal objectives in the way we have described is an overwhelming one.

We do not imagine that either the administrative or the distributional implications of these proposals could be absorbed rapidly. But we have shown that it is possible to reduce social security expenditure and at the same time improve the position of the worse off by increasing the efficiency of the benefit system. It is simply not the case that help for the poor requires additional public spending, or that public-spending reductions must necessarily hit those in low incomes.

Although we are putting forward objectives rather than a specific package, we have nevertheless been careful to analyse proposals in a carefully costed framework of neutrality. We have not adopted any of the sleights of hand which are commonly used by social security reformers attempting to balance their books. We have assumed benefits and tax allowances fully indexed from present levels. We have assumed that relief for mortgage interest, pension funds, and insurance continues at the present level. We have not anticipated any of the additional resources that economic growth resulting from a better tax and benefit system or from other policies might bring about. We have not found money from reductions in other areas of public expenditure. We have not used any of the additional revenue which the Government has committed itself to provide for social security benefits as the State Earnings-Related Pension Scheme develops. The measures we have put forward have at least one evident disadvantage. We acknowledge that substantial numbers of people lose from the changes that we propose. This is, of course, an inevitable characteristic of any reform. It is true that the losers are principally well-off households which lose access to benefits or tax allowances that they do not need. It is also true that it is these households which will gain most from lower taxes, both in cash terms and as a result of the incentive effects of lower rates. But the fact that people do not need the benefits which they receive does not imply that they do not wish to go on receiving them. If history is any guide, it is very likely that we will continue with an ineffective and costly system because politicians are too timid to contemplate substantive reform; but we have not been constrained by what is 'politically possible'. The boundaries of what is 'politically possible' rarely reflect more than the limited horizons of current politicians or, more commonly, current administrators. History abounds with examples of where yesterday's political impossibility is today's agenda for debate and tomorrow's conventional wisdom. The opportunity for the presentation and the rapid implementation of the Beveridge Report came from the break in continuity provided by the Second World War; peacetime change occurs, perhaps unfortunately, more slowly.

References and notes

1. This move has been widely canvassed in recent years, particularly following the publication of a Government Green Paper (*The Taxation of Husband and Wife,* Cmnd. 8693, London, HMSO, 1981). For a summary of the arguments see C.N. Morris and N.A. Warren, 'The Taxation of the Family', *Fiscal Studies* 2/1 (March 1981).
2. *The Structure of Personal Income Taxation and Income Support* (report of a sub-committee to the Treasury and Civil Service Select Committee), London, HMSO (May 1983).

Appendix: Old and new systems compared

Income tax

OLD (1983/4 Tax levels, Post-November Benefits)	NEW
Personal allowance of tax-free income: £1,785 p.a. (single) £2,795 p.a. (couple)	Replaced by a non-refundable tax credit of £450 p.a. per individual.
Working wives allowed additional single allowance. One-parent families treated as couple. Over-65s allowed an additional £575 p.a. (single). £960 p.a. (couple), of tax-free income, tapered away if total income exceeds £7,600 p.a. (the 'age allowance').	
Mortgage interest allowed as full deduction. Life insurance relief allowed at 15% [1983/4 system abolished for 1984/5]. Pension contributions deductible, some receipts tax-free.	Unchanged. Additional tax credits granted equal to 30% of deductible amount, or higher for higher-rate taxpayer. Life insurance relief allowed at 15%.
Liability assessed on cumulative basis. Partial coverage of tax returns.	Changed to system of end-year assessment. All individuals receive tax returns every year.
Self-employed taxed on preceding-year basis.	Self-employed treated as other individuals on current-year basis.
Basic rate of tax 0.30	

Higher rates:

Band of taxable income* (£ p.a.)	Rate
14,801–17,200	0.40
17,201–21,800	0.45
21,801–28,900	0.50
28,901–36,000	0.55
Over 36,001	0.60

* Taxable income is total income less personal allowances.

National insurance contributions

Those with earnings below £32.50 p.w. unaffected.

Those with earnings above £32.50 p.a. pay:

	If not contracted-out of SERPS	If contracted-out of SERPS
On first £32.50	0.09	0.09
£32.50-£235	0.09	0.0685
On income over £235	zero	zero

Self-employed and voluntary special (Classes 2, 3, 4) contributions regimes.

Replaced by combined income tax and national insurance rate structure:

On all income up to £17,600 p.a.	0.34
On income £17,601–£24,600 p.a.	0.45
On income £24,601–£31,700 p.a.	0.50
On income £31,701–£38,800 p.a.	0.55
Over £38,800	0.60

No special regimes.

	NEW
OLD	
(1983/4 Tax levels, Post-November Benefits)	

Employers pay on their employees' behalf:

	If not contracted-out of SERPS	If contracted-out of SERPS
On first £32.50	0.1045	0.1045
£32.50–£235	0.1045	0.0635
On income over £235	zero	zero

Replaced by single payroll tax of 0.10.

Rebate payable to recognised occupational pension schemes through PAYE equivalent to 14 per cent of total tax payments (not including withdrawal) up to a ceiling of £500 per individual employee.

Child benefit

Payable for all children, regardless of parents' income, at £6.50 p.w.

Additional payment for one-parent families £4.05 p.w.

Family income supplement

For those with incomes below an income limit of £85.50 p.w. with one child (plus £9.50 for each subsequent child):

50% of difference between income and income limit, subject to maximum payment of £22 p.w. (plus £2 for each subsequent child).

Income for family income supplement payments does not include receipts of child benefit or housing benefit.

Replaced by single benefit credit and withdrawal system for working families:

£20 p.w. (single)
£30 p.w. (couple)

plus £35.50 for the first child if any child under 5
£28.50 for the first child if all over 5

Housing benefit

Calculate a 'needs allowance' (NA) of:

£43.05 (single)
£63.50 (couple)
plus £11.90 per child
plus £ 5.50 for each subsequent child
plus 80% housing costs
less 50% of all income (other than benefit credit) for
families with children
25% of all income for others.

If result negative, no payment occurs.

A separate scheme applies to one-parent families and to
pensioners (see below).

Deduct disregards of £17.45 head earnings, £5 for
secondary earner, from income to give (Y).

Then housing benefit for non-pensioners is 60%
of rent payments *plus* 25% of (NA$-Y$) if Y is below
NA or *minus* 21% of ($Y-$NA) if Y is above NA,
**and 60% of rates payments *plus* 8% of (NA$-Y$)
if Y is below NA or *minus* 7% of ($Y-$NA) if
Y is above NA.**

Housing benefit for pensioners is 60% of
rent payments *plus* 50% of (NA$-Y$) if Y is below
NA or *minus* 20% of ($Y-$NA) if Y is above NA,
**and 60% of rates payments *plus* 20% of (NA$-Y$)
if Y is below NA or *minus* 7% of ($Y-$NA) if Y
is above NA.**

Housing benefit payment for rent cannot be less than
£0.20 or more than £35 or more than rent payments.

Housing benefit payment for rates cannot be less
than £0.10 or more than £8 or more than rates
payments.

Income for housing benefit purposes includes family
income supplement and child benefit.

OLD	NEW
(1983/4 Tax levels, Post-November Benefits)	

Benefit in kind

Recipients of family income supplement and supplementary benefit (and certificated housing benefit) qualify automatically for:

    free milk and vitamins (pregnancy, nursing, young children);

    free school meals;

    free prescriptions;

    refund of hospital fares;

    free spectacles (NHS);

    free dental treatment (NHS).

Each of these benefits has its own means test and/or is available to some categories of people irrespective of income.

Free school meals discontinued.

Other benefits in kind administered by new local advisory offices. Available to all those receiving partial net benefit credit with no withdrawal. For those not receiving net benefit credit, the value of benefits in kind received is added as a notional amount to their benefit credit and withdrawn in the usual way.

Unemployment benefit

Weekly, flat-rate benefit of:

    £27.05 (single)

    £43.75 (couple)

    plus £ 0.15 for each dependent child.

Replaced by single non-withdrawable, taxable benefit credit for the unemployed and sick:

    £27.05 p.w. (single)

    £43.75 p.w. (couple).

Entitlement by contributions condition, dependent on having contributed on the basis of at least the lower earnings limit (currently £32.50) for 50 weeks in a year some 1–3 years previously.

Paid for up to 52 weeks in any spell (spells may be linked).

Sickness benefit

Entitlement and rates as for unemployment benefit.

Receipt requires doctor's certificate.

Paid for up to 28 weeks.

From April 1983, employers responsible for first 8 weeks.

Supplementary benefit

Payable if a combination of national insurance benefits (unemployment benefit, sick benefit, retirement pension, child benefit, housing benefit, etc.) is not sufficient to bring 'resources' (income plus other benefits) to cover 'needs'.

'Needs' for the unemployed and sick are determined by the following short-term 'scale rates', irrespective of period of receipt:

£26.80 p.w. (single)
£43.50 p.w. (couple

In addition, the unemployed and sick receive a withdrawable benefit credit of:

£13.70 for each child 11–15
£ 9.15 for each child 0–10
plus the full amount of housing costs

less 25% of other income if no children
or 50% of other income if children.

OLD	NEW
(1983/4 Tax levels, Post-November Benefits)	

OLD column:

plus £13.70 for each child 11–15
£ 9.15 for each child 0–10

plus, for each person living in the household:

£21.45 aged 18 or over
£16.50 aged 16–17.

If resources are less than needs, then the difference is available as supplementary benefit.

In addition, supplementary benefit payments are sometimes made to cover exceptional needs such as large heating bills, or to purchase durables and clothing.

Retirement pension

Weekly flat rate of:

£34.05 (single)
£54.50 (couple)
plus £ 7.60 for each dependent child.

Entitlement is by contribution condition.

This is quite complicated, but attempts to ensure that the individual has made minimum contributions for most of his/her working life.

Supplementary benefit (pensioners)

Supplementary benefit for pensioners (and invalids and

NEW column:

Exceptional needs payments now administered by the new local advisory offices.

Replaced by single taxable benefit credit and withdrawal system for pensioners:

£80 p.w. (single)
£115 p.w. (couple)
plus (non-taxable) additions for dependent children and working families
plus 80% of housing costs (non-taxable)
less 20% of all income, including single or couple benefit credit.

'Reckonable earnings' for the purposes of the State-the long-term sick) is determined as described above, except that the long-term scale rate now applies:

£34.10 p.w. (single)
£54.55 p.w. (couple)

In addition, pensioners receive assistance with their housing payments in full if they have no other income, or as described above if they have income on top of the state pension.

Earnings-Related Pension Scheme replaced by calculation based upon tax (but not withdrawal) position. New 'reckonable earnings' are now calculated as 2.95 times tax payment up to a maximum of £12,000 per year.

One-parent families

Receive child benefit and one-parent benefit.

Those with no other income receive supplementary benefit at the rate for a couple, with additions for children as indicated above. As a special concession, one-parent families are allowed to earn £20 (on top of the £4 disregard) which is only withdrawn from their supplementary benefit at a 0.5 rate.

They may choose to receive family income supplement instead, if this is beneficial, provided they work for more than 24 hours in a week.

Replaced by single benefit credit and withdrawal system for one-parent families:

£20 per week
plus £5.85 one-parent addition
plus increases for children as working family
plus 80% of housing costs

less 50% of all income.

Other benefits

These include a number of non-contributory and contributory benefits for the disabled, for industrial injuries, for maternity, for death, for pensioners, and so on.

Integration into the new system is not considered in this book. However, the payment method for the benefits described above could be adapted to cover most benefits, with variable need covered by variable benefit credit amounts. Benefits to the disabled could remain as non-withdrawable payments.

Glossary

This glossary attempts to define for the non-technical reader various technical or administrative terms which are used in the text but not adequately defined there. The glossary is arranged in alphabetical order.

Absolute Poverty
'Poverty' based upon a 'subsistence' level of income.

Actuarially calculated
Contributions would be set equal to precisely that amount which, on the balance of probabilities about mortality, inflation, and so on, would exactly yield enough (including investment at a prescribed real interest rate) to pay the promised benefits.

Age allowance
Persons over 65, or a couple where one partner is over 65, are allowed a larger tax allowance. In 1983/4 these were £2,360 for a single person and £3,755 for a couple.

Benefits in kind
Used to refer to benefits which are received in non-monetary form, such as free school meals, free welfare milk, or free prescriptions.

Black economy
A general, and usually imperfectly defined, term used to identify those activities which are unrecorded for tax or benefit purposes.

Clawback
All taxpayer recipients of family allowances were charged an amount of tax which removed some of their entitlement. In 1976, this amounted to £1 per week.

Contingent
Benefits whose payment is based on the occurrence of an event, such as old age, or unemployment, and is not dependent on evidence of need or hardship.

Cumulative
Income tax in the UK, unlike most other countries, is administered on a 'cumulative' basis. This means that deductions are based on earnings in the tax year to date, and not just on the month of payment.

Dietary
The scale of food requirements needed for subsistence.

Direct tax
Examples in the UK are income tax or national insurance contributions; a tax which is levied directly on income.

152

Disregard	An amount of earnings or other income which is not taken into account when calculating entitlement to benefit.
Earnings-related supplement	Between 1966 and 1982, recipients of unemployment and sickness benefits received, in addition to their flat-rate benefit, an amount related to previous earnings.
Fiscal year	The period of time used for calculating tax liability and for Government accounting purposes. In the UK it runs from 6 April to 5 April.
Flat rate	A benefit payment which consists of a single payment, independent of income, is known as a flat-rate benefit.
Friendly Society	These emerged in the eighteenth and nineteenth centuries as self-help organisations for groups of workers. In a typical scheme, workers would contribute to a central fund from which benefits would be paid for less-fortunate members.
Funded	One of the two methods of financing a pension scheme. Contributions may be paid into a central fund, which is then invested and pensions paid from the proceeds. Or the scheme may be 'pay as you go', in which case current contributions are used to pay current pensions. All UK state schemes have in reality been of the second kind.
Graduated	In the first post-war scheme, both contributions and benefits were flat rate. In 1961, the scheme was extended so that contributions became related to income, or graduated, and eventual pensions reflected income during the insured person's lifetime.
Hierarchical	In this context, used to indicate a 'pyramidal' structure. Low-level units (local offices) are linked to regional computers which are in turn linked together.
Hypothecated	A hypothecated tax is one the revenue from which is strictly reserved for a particular use.
Incentives	Usually used to describe the likelihood of an individual taking work or earning additional money. Incentives to work are affected by both tax rates and reductions in benefit; if the amount of any additional earnings which is retained is very low (i.e. the 'marginal rate' is high) then it is less likely that the individual will undertake the additional work.
Income-related benefit	A benefit whose amount is reduced as the other income of the recipient rises.
Investment income surcharge	In 1983/4, all non-earned income in excess of £7,100 is subject to an additional tax rate of 15 per cent.

Less eligibility	A principle intended to minimise the disincentive effect of social benefits. Under it, no unemployed men should receive a higher standard of living than the poorest working men can achieve.
Lump-sum payment	A payment of a given amount which is paid to everyone, irrespective of income or other characteristics.
Marginal rate	The proportion of additional earnings taken in tax.
Married man's allowance	The additional allowance given to a man if he is married. At present (1983/4), the single tax allowance is £1,785, and the allowance for a married man £2,795, a difference of £1,010 and worth £303 per year (£5.83 per week) to a basic-rate taxpayer.
Means-tested	Entitlement depends on other resources available to the benefit unit. The test is normally based on income, but may also involve capital and other resources.
Movements operation	Because PAYE is administered cumulatively, it is necessary to trace an individual, week by week, if he moves jobs. It is also necessary to link couples where the partners are employed in different geographical areas. The resulting flow of paper is termed the PAYE 'movements operation'.
National insurance fund	The fund into which contributions are paid and from which national insurance benefits are financed.
Negative income tax	Used to describe a system whereby the tax system is used both to pay money to those with low incomes and to take money from those with high incomes. The proposals put forward in this book are a type of negative income tax, as are social dividend schemes and the tax credit scheme of 1972.
Net income distribution	Net income here refers to family income after receipt of all benefits and deductions of income tax and national insurance contributions.
Non-contributory	Financed direct from tax revenue and payable without conditions based on a contribution record.
Notice of coding	All PAYE taxpayers are sent a 'notice of coding' every year which informs them of the allowances which will be credited against their tax liability.
P60	The Inland Revenue form which is used to advise employees of their recorded incomes and tax payments during a fiscal year.
Passport benefits	Benefits in kind (see page 000) are available automatically to the recipients of family income supplement or supplementary benefit. This is known as the 'passport' system.
PAYE	Pay As You Earn is the mechanism whereby most

income tax is collected in the UK. Under PAYE, income tax is deducted from gross income by employers, who then pay a net-of-tax amount to their employees.

Period of assessment
The period over which income tax is recorded for the purposes of determining tax liability or benefit entitlement.

Poverty
Poverty is rarely precisely defined. In many of the post-war poverty studies, being 'poor' is equated with having an income below the national assistance/supplementary benefit level or some multiple of it. In nineteenth-century studies, 'poverty' meant having insufficient income to achieve a certain 'subsistence' level of consumption. Recent works (for example P. Townsend, *Poverty in the United Kingdom*, Harmondsworth, Penguin, 1979) suggest a more subtle definition: 'poverty' is the inability to behave in a similar way to one's peers.

Poverty trap
In its most severe form, the 'poverty trap' means that poor working families can end up worse off if they earn additional income. The 'marginal rate' they face can be in excess of 100 per cent if they pay tax (30 per cent) and national insurance (9 per cent), and receive family income supplement (withdrawn at 50 per cent) and housing benefit (between 28 per cent and 33 per cent).

Outdoor relief
As the Poor Law developed, conditions emerged under which money would be paid to the poor — principally the elderly — without it being necessary for them to move into the workhouse.

Qualifying earnings
Those earnings between the lower and upper earnings limits which determine pension entitlement.

Refundable
A tax credit is said to be 'refundable' if it can be used even if there is no tax liability. Our 'benefit credit' is thus a refundable tax credit.

Relative poverty
'Poverty' based upon some proportion of the standard of living of the population as a whole.

Replacement rate
The ratio of an individual's income when out of work to that when in work. In practice, measuring this is complicated by the peculiar pattern of benefit receipt and tax refunds, etc. See A.W. Dilnot and C.N. Morris ('The Private Costs and Benefits of Unemployment', *Oxford Economic Papers*, November 1983) for a discussion.

Resources
The term used for the income available to a family. If 'needs' as defined for supplementary benefit are less than 'resources', then the family is entitled to benefit.

Revenue-neutral	This means that the increases or decreases in expenditure implied by the new policy will be balanced by increases or decreases in tax revenue.
Schedule	Income tax is administered under a series of 'schedules' dependent on the kind of income. The two most important are Schedule E (income from employment) and Schedule D (income from self-employment).
Social insurance	This is the term generally used for schemes such as those proposed in the Beveridge Report, where members of society pay a flat amount in return for a promise of benefits if certain things — like unemployment, becoming sick, or old age — happen to them.
Subsistence income	The amount of income required to provide a family with a nutritionally adequate diet, basic shelter, and warmth. The generosity of calculations of 'subsistence' increased from the nineteenth to the twentieth century, with the post-war estimates allowing for some items which were not absolutely necessary to keep the family alive.
Supplementary benefit scale rate	The requirements for a family of a particular size, with particular ages of children, are specified, for supplementary benefit purposes in its 'scale rate'.
Tax liability	The amount of tax which an individual has to pay, given his income and other circumstances.
Temperance society	This provided assistance for the destitute from funds provided by philanthropic individuals. This name emerged because conditions of abstinence were imposed on recipients.
Topping-up	The process whereby receipt of benefit is brought to the family's full entitlement by the addition of small amounts of another benefit, typically supplementary benefit or housing benefit.
Unemployment trap	The problem that individuals can be 'better off on the dole'. If a family man earns a very low wage, the benefits he would get if unemployed can exceed his net income in work. The problem occurs because benefits are paid to cover need such as families or housing — while wages are not.
Unfunded liabilities	The liabilities of a pension scheme which are not strictly covered by the fund accumulated by that scheme.
Uprating	Every November, benefits are 'uprated' in order to keep their value in line with the rise in prices. The basis on which this is done has been varied several times in the last few years.

Wage-stop   This mechanism was applied to unemployment benefit in the post-war period. Under it, unemployment assistance was not permitted to be higher than the recipient could be expected to earn in work.

Workhouse   The nineteenth-century institution set aside for the destitute. In exchange for a roof, and basic food, able-bodied people were expected to perform menial tasks, often for long hours.

Select Bibliography

Abel-Smith, B. and Townsend, P., *New Pensions for the Old*, Fabian Research Series No. 171, London, Fabian Society (March 1955).

Abel-Smith, B. and Townsend, P., *The Poor and the Poorest*, London, G. Bell (1965).

Atkinson, A. B., *Poverty in Britain and the Reform of Social Security*, Cambridge, Cambridge University Press (1969).

Atkinson, A. B., 'Policies for Poverty', *Lloyds Bank Review* (April 1971).

Atkinson, A. B., *The Economics of Inequality*, London, Oxford University Press (1975).

Atkinson, A. B., *The Distribution of Income and Wealth in Britain*, London, Allen and Unwin (1976).

Atkinson, A. B. and Flemming, J. S., 'Unemployment, Social Security and Disincentives', *Midland Bank Review* (Autumn 1978).

Atkinson, A. B., Maynard, A. K., and Trinder, C. G., 'National Assistance and Low Incomes in 1950', *Social Policy and Administration*, 15 (1981), 10–31.

Atkinson, J. A., 'The Developing Relationship Between the State Pension Scheme and Occupational Pensions', *Social and Economic Administration*, 11/3 (1977).

Austin, M. and Posnett, J., 'The Charity Sector in England and Wales – Characteristics and Public Accountability', *National Westminster Bank Quarterly*, 281 (August 1979).

Bagley, C., *The Cost of a Child: Problems in the Relief and Measurement of Poverty*, London, Institute of Psychiatry (1969).

Beckerman, W., 'The Impact of Income Maintenance Payments on Poverty in Britain', *Economic Journal* (June 1970).

Beckerman, W. and Clark, S., *Poverty and Social Security in Britain since 1961*, London, Institute for Fiscal Studies (1982).

Beveridge, W. H., *Unemployment, A Problem of Industry*, London, Aberdeen Press (1909).

Beveridge, W. H., *Full Employment in a Free Society*, London (1944).

Booth, C., *Old Age Pensions and the Aged Poor*, London, Macmillan (1889).

Booth, C., *Pauperism: A Picture* and *The Endowment of Old Age: An Argument*, London, Macmillan (1892).

Booth, C., *The Condition of the Aged Poor*, London, Macmillan (1894).

Booth, C., *The Life and Labour of the People in London* (17-vol. edition), London, Macmillan (1902–4). (Original volume on East London published 1889).

Briggs, A., *A Study of the Work of Seebohm Rowntree*, London, Longman (1961).

Brown, C. V. and Dawson, D. A., 'Personal Taxation, Incentives and Tax Reform', PEP Broadsheet 506, London (1968).

Brown, J. C., *Low Pay and Poverty in the United Kingdom*, London, Policy Studies Institute (1981).

Bruce, M., *The Coming of the Welfare State*, London, Batsford (1961).

Canadian Council for Social Development, 'Guaranteed Annual Income: An Integral Approach', Ottawa (1973).

Carter, C., 'The Priorities of Public Expenditure', *Policy Studies*, 1/2 (1980).

Carter, C. and Wilson, T., 'Discussing the Welfare State', Discussion Paper No. 1, London, Policy Studies Institute (1980).

Christopher, A. *et al.*, 'Policy for Poverty', Report of the Institute of Economic Affairs Study Groups, London, IEA (1970).

Cole, G. D. H., *The Post-war Condition of Britain*, London, Routledge and Kegan Paul (1956).

Collard, D., *Altriusm and Economy*, Oxford, Martin Robertson (1978).

Cooper, M. H. (ed.), *Social Policy: A Survey of Recent Developments*, Oxford, Blackwell (1974).

Creedy, J., *State Pensions in Britain*, London, National Institute of Economic and Social Research (1982).

Creedy, J. (ed.), *The Economics of Unemployment in Britain*, London, Butterworth (1981).

Culyer, A. J., *The Political Economy of Social Policy*, Oxford, Martin Robertson (1980).

de Schweinitz, K., *England's Road to Social Security*, New York, Perpetua (1961).

Diamond, P. A., 'Negative Taxes and the Poverty Problem — A Review Article', *National Tax Journal* (September 1968).

Dilnot, A. W. and Morris, C. N., 'What Do We Know About the Black Economy?', *Fiscal Studies*, 2/1 (March 1981).

Dilnot, A. W. and Morris, C. N., 'Private Costs and Benefits of Unemployment: Measuring Replacement Rates', in C. A. Greenhalgh, P. R. G. Layard, and A. J. Oswald (eds.), *The Causes of Unemployment*, Oxford University Press (1984).

Donnison, D., *Housing Policy Since the War*, Welwyn, Codicote Press (1962).

Donnison, D., *The Government of Housing*, Harmondsworth, Penguin Books (1967).

Doran, A., Shanui, N., and Tanir, Y., 'Income Maintenance from a Family Policy Perspective: Description and Analysis of Programmes in Israel', Hebrew University (1981).

Ermisch, J., 'Paying the Piper: Demographic Changes and Pension Contributions', *Policy Studies*, 1 (1981).

Feinstein, C. H., *Statistical Tables of National Income, Expenditure and Output 1855-1956*, Cambridge (1976).

Ferner, L., Kornbluh, J., and Hahner, A., *Poverty in America*, Ann Arbor, Michigan University Press (1965).

Fiegehen, G. C. and Lansley, P. S., 'The Tax Credit Proposals', *National Institute Economic Review* (May 1973).

Fiegehen, G. C., Lansley, P. S., and Smith, A. D., *Poverty and Progress in Britain 1953-73*, National Institute of Economic and Social Research Occasional Paper No. 29, Cambridge, Cambridge University Press (1977).

Field, F., Meacher, M., and Pond, C., *To Him Who Hath*, Harmondsworth, Penguin Books (1977).

Forder, A., *Concepts in Social Administration*, London, Routledge and Kegan Paul (1974).

Fraser, D., *The Evolution of the British Welfare State*, London, Macmillan (1973).

George, V., *Social Security: Beveridge and After*, London, Routledge and Kegan Paul (1976).

Gilbert, B., *The Evolution of National Insurance in Great Britain*, London, Michael Joseph (1966).

Gilbert, B., *British Social Policy 1914-1939*, London, Batsford (1970).

Gosden, P. H. J. H., *Self-Help: Voluntary Associations in Nineteenth-Century Britain*, London, Batsford (1974).

Gough, I., *The Political Economy of the Welfare State*, London, Macmillan (1979).

Green, C., *Negative Taxes and the Poverty Problem*, Washington DC, Brookings Institution (1967).

Hall, P., Land, H., Parker, R., and Webb, A., *Change, Choice and Conflict in Social Policy*, London (1975).

Harris, A., *Social Welfare of the Aged*, London, HMSO (1968).

Harris, J., *Unemployment and Politics*, Oxford University Press (1972).

Harris, J., *William Beveridge*, Oxford University Press (1977).

Hay, J., *The Origins of the Liberal Social Welfare Reforms: 1906-1914*, London (1975).

Health and Social Security, Department of, *Report by the Government Actuary on the Financial Provisions of the National Superannuation and Social Insurance Bill*, Cmnd. 4223, London, HMSO (1969).

Health and Social Security, Department of, *Operational Strategy: A Framework for the Future*, London, HMSO (1982).

Hemming, R. and Kay, J. A., 'Occupational Pension Schemes: Problems and Reform' (mimeo), London, Institute for Fiscal Studies (1981).

Hemming, R. and Kay, J. A., 'The Costs of the State Earnings-Related Pension Scheme', Working Paper No. 21, London, Institute for Fiscal Studies (1981).

Hemming, R. and Kay, J. A., 'The Costs of the State Earnings Related Pension Scheme', *Economic Journal* (June 1982).

Hemming, R. and Kay, J. A., 'Contracting Out of the State Earnings Related Pension Scheme', Fiscal Studies, 2/3.

Howe, J. R., *Two-Parent Families: A Study of Their Resources and Needs in 1968, 1969 and 1970*. Statistical Report Series No. 14, London, HMSO (1971).

Institute for Economic Affairs, 'Policy for Poverty', IEA Research Monograph 20, London (1970).

Institute for Fiscal Studies, 'Proceedings of the Conference on the Proposals for a Tax Credit System' London, IFS (1973).

Jackson, D., *Poverty*, Macmillan Studies in Economics, London, Macmillan (1972).

Jenkins, S. P. and Maynard, A. K., 'The Rowntree Surveys: Poverty in York Since 1899', in C. H. Feinstein (ed.), *York 1831-1981*, York, William Sessions (1981).

Judge, K., 'Beveridge: Past, Present and Future', in C. Sandford, C. Pond, and R. Walker (eds.), *Taxation and Social Policy*, London, Heinemann (1980).

Kaldor, N., 'A Critique of the Green Paper Proposals', in Minutes of *Evidence to the Select Committee on Tax Credit*, H.C. 341 (March 1973).

Kay, J. A. and King, M. A., *The British Tax System* (3rd edition), Oxford, Oxford University Press (1983).

Kay, J. A., 'The Effects of Raising Tax Allowances', *Fiscal Studies* 5/1 (February 1984).

Kincaid, J. C., *Poverty and Equality in Britain*, Harmondsworth, Penguin Books (1973).

King, M. A. and Atkinson, A. B., 'Housing Policy Taxation and Reform', *Midland Bank Review* (Spring 1980).

Kinnersly, P., *The Hazards of Work: How to Fight Them*, Workers' Handbook No. 1, London, Pluto Press (1973).

Lambert, N. A. D. and Matthewman, J., *Social Security and State Benefits 1982/3* Croydon, Tolley Publishing Company (1983).

Lansley, S., 'What Hope for the Poor?', *Lloyds Bank Review*, 132 (April 1979).

Layard, R., Piachaud, D., and Stewart, M., 'The Causes of Poverty', background paper for *Sixth Report of the Royal Commission on the Distribution of Income and Wealth*, Cmnd. 7175, London, HMSO (1978).

Lees, D., 'Poor Families and Fiscal Reform', *Lloyds Bank Review* (October 1967).

Levitan, S. A., *Programs in Aid of the Poor for the 1980's,* Baltimore and London, Johns Hopkins University Press (1980).

Levy, H., *National Health Insurance: a Critical Study,* Cambridge, NIESR (1944).

Lister, R., *The Take-up of Means Tested Benefits,* London, Child Poverty Action Group (1974).

Lister, R., *Social Security: The Case for Reform,* London, Child Poverty Action Group (1975).

Lynes, T., *Social Security and Poverty in the UK,* London, Policy Studies Institute (1981).

Lynes, T., *The Penguin Guide to Supplementary Benefits,* Harmondsworth, Penguin Books (1981).

Marshall, T., *Social Policy in the Twentieth Century* (4th edition), London, Hutchinson (1975).

Marshall, T. H., *Social Policy in the Twentieth Century* (4th edition), London, Hutchinson (1977).

McClements, L., *The Economics of Social Security,* London (1978).

Meade, J. E., *The Structure and Reform of Direct Taxation* (report of Institute for Fiscal Studies committee under the chairmanship of J. E. Meade), London, Allen and Unwin (1978).

Micklethwaite, Sir R. G., *The National Insurance Commissioners,* London, Hamlyn (1976).

Minford, A. P. L., *Unemployment: Cause and Cure,* Oxford, Martin Robertson (1982).

Morris, C. N., 'The Structure of Personal Income Taxation and Income Support', *Fiscal Studies,* 3/3 (November 1982).

Munnell, A. H., *The Future of Social Security,* Washington DC, Brookings Institution (1977).

National Assistance Board, *Homeless Single Persons,* London, HMSO (1966).

National Association of Pension Funds, *Survey of Occupational Pension Schemes 1980,* London, NAPF (1981).

National Consumer Council, *Means Tested Benefits,* London, NCC, (1977).

Nicholson, J. L., 'The Redistribution of Income', in A. B. Atkinson (ed.), *The Personal Distribution of Income,* London, Allen and Unwin (1976).

Ogus, A. I., 'Great Britain', in P. A. Kohler and H. F. Zacher (eds.), *The Evolution of Social Insurance,* London, Frances Pinter (1982).

O'Higgins, M. and Ruggles, P., 'The Distribution of Public Expenditure and Taxes among Households in the United Kingdom', *Income and Wealth* (September 1981).

Orshansky, M., 'Counting the Poor: Another Look at the Poverty Profile', *Social Security Bulletin,* 28 (January 1965).

Orshansky, M., 'How Poverty is Measured', *Monthly Labor Review* (February 1969).

Parker, H., *The Moral Hazard of Social Security Benefits,* London, Institute for Economic Affairs (1982).

Parker, R. A., 'Social Administration and Scarcity', in E. Butterworth and R. Holman (eds.), *Social Welfare in Modern Britain,* London, Fontana (1975).

Partington, T. M. and Jowell, J., *Welfare Law and Policy,* New York (1979).

Pechman, J. A., Aaron, H. J. and Taussig, M. K., *Social Security: Perspectives for Reform,* Washington DC, Brookings Institution (1968).

Pigou, A. C., *Economics of Welfare,* London, Macmillan (1920).

Pinker, R., *Social Theory and Social Policy,* London, Heinemann (1971).

Plattner, M. F., 'The Welfare State v. the Redistributive State', *Public Interest,* 55 (1979).

Polanyi, G. and Polanyi, P., 'Tax Credits: A Reverse Income Tax', *National Westminster Bank Quarterly Review* (February 1973).

Prest, A. R., 'The Negative Income Tax: Concepts and Problems', *British Tax Review* (November–December 1970).

Pringle, M. K., *The Needs of Children* (2nd edition), London, Hutchinson (1980).

Rhys-Williams, B., 'The New Social Contrast', Conservative Political Centre (1967).

Rhys-Williams, B., in *Minutes of Evidence to the Select Committee on Tax Credit*, H.C. 341-II (1973).

Rhys-Williams, Lady T., 'Something to Look Forward to', MacDonald (1943).

Richardson, J. H., *Economic and Financial Aspects of Social Security*, London (1960).

Robson, W. A., *Welfare State and Welfare Society*, London, Allen and Unwin (1976).

Rose, H., *The Housing Problem*, London, Heinemann (1968).

Rose, M. E., *The Relief of Poverty: 1834-1914*, London, Macmillan (1972).

Rowntree, B. S., *Poverty: A Study of Town Life*, London and New York, Macmillan (1902).

Rowntree, B. S., *The Human Needs of Labour*, London, Nelson (1918); revised edition, London, Longman Green (1937).

Rowntree, B. S., *Poverty and Progress: A Second Social Survey of York*, London, New York, and Toronto; Longman Green (1941).

Rowntree, B. S. and Lasker, B., *Unemployment: A Social Survey*, London, Macmillan (1911).

Rowntree, B. S. and Lavers, G. R., *Poverty and the Welfare State*, London, New York, and Toronto, Longman Green (1951).

Royal Commission on the Distribution of Income and Wealth, Report No. 6, *Lower Incomes*, Cmnd. 7175, London, HMSO (1978).

Ruggles, P. and O'Higgins, M., 'The Distribution of Public Expenditure and Taxes Among Households in the United States', *Review of Income and Wealth*, 2 (1981).

Sandford, C., 'Taxation and Social Policy: An Overview', in C. Sandford, C. Pond, and R. Walker (eds.), *Taxation and Social Policy*, London, Heinemann (1980).

Seers, D., *Changes in the Cost of Living and the Distribution of Income Since 1938*, Oxford, Blackwell (1949).

Seers, D., *The Levelling of Incomes Since 1938*, Oxford, Blackwell (1957).

Seldon, A., *Whither the Welfare State?* London, Institute of Economic Affairs (1981).

Shanas, E., Townsend, P., and Wedderburn, D., *Living Conditions of the Aged in Three Industrial Societies*, London, Routledge and Kegan Paul (1968).

Sleeman, J. F., *Resources for the Welfare State*, London, Longman (1979).

Social Security, Ministry of, *Administration of the Wage Stop*, London, HMSO (1967).

Thane, P. (ed.), *The Origins of British Social Policy*, London (1978).

Thompson, L. H., 'The Social Security Reform Debate', *Journal of Economic Literature*, 21 (December 1983), 1425–67.

Tillyard, Sir F. *Unemployment Insurance in Great Britain 1911-1948*, Leigh-on-Sea (1949).

Titmuss, R. M., *Essays on the Welfare State*, London, Allen and Unwin (1958).

Titmuss, R. M., *Income Distribution and Social Change*, London, Allen and Unwin (1962).

Tobin, J., Pechman, J. A., and Mieszkowski, P. M., *Is a Negative Income Tax Practical?*, Washington DC, Brookings Institution (1967).

Townsend, P., 'Poverty: Ten Years After Beveridge', *Political and Economic Planning*, 19/344 (1952).

Townsend, P. and Wedderburn, D., *The Aged in the Welfare State*, London, G. Bell (1965).

Townsend, P., *The Concept of Poverty*, London, Heinemann (1970).
Townsend, P., *Poverty in the United Kingdom*, Harmondsworth, Penguin (1979).
Townsend, P. and Wedderburn, D., *The Aged in the Welfare State*, London, G. Bell (1965).
Walley, J., *Social Security: Another British Failure*, London, Knight (1972).
Webb, S. and Webb, B., *English Poor Law History Part II, The Last 100 Years*, Edinburgh (1929).
Williams, F. (ed.), *Why the Poor Pay More*, London, National Consumer Council (1977).
Willis, J. R. M. and Hardwick, P. J. W., *Tax Expenditure in the United Kingdom*, London, Institute of Fiscal Studies (1978).
Wilson, T. (ed.), *Pensions, Inflation and Growth*, London, Heinemann (1974).
Wilson, T. and Wilson, D. J., *The Political Economy of the Welfare State*, London, Allen and Unwin (1982).

Index